MIDPOINT KEYS TO CHIRON

by Chris Brooks

AMERICAN FEDERATION OF ASTROLOGERS, INC.
P O BOX 22040
TEMPE, AZ 85285-2040

ISBN: 0-86690-407-7
LCC Number: 91-77411

First Printing: 1992
Second Printing: 1996

Cover Design: Lynda Kay Fullerton

Published by:
American Federation of Astrologers, Inc.
PO Box 22040
6535 S. Rural Road
Tempe, AZ 85285-2040

Printed in the United States of America

TABLE OF CONTENTS

List of Figures

PREFACE

This volume is a compilation of many years research and an attempt to share with others the information gleaned about two of the most important and exciting topics to appear in the field of astrology this century — cosmobiology and the newly discovered planetary body, Chiron. Cosmobiology is a term used by researchers like the German Reinhold Ebertin, to describe this new science which seeks to understand how the laws of the heavens affect those on earth. Like physics and chemistry which try to unlock the laws and secrets of the material universe, cosmobiology seeks to understand scientifically the relationship between man and the cosmos.

Chris Brooks

Abbreviations Used in Text

SU - Sun

MO - Moon

ME - Mercury

VE - Venus

MA - Mars

JU - Jupiter

SA - Saturn

UR - Uranus

NE - Neptune

PL - Pluto

CH - Chiron

M - Midheaven

A - Ascendant

MN - North Node of the Moon

CSI - The Combination of Stellar Influences

$_s$ - directed planet

$_t$ - transiting

1

Chiron – For Signs and For Seasons

"And they shall bring about the
seasons on the earth and mark
the days and the years."
Genesis 1:15

Discovery

After many years of study in this field of astrology I tend to look askance at anything new until I've studied it a long time and proven to myself that it has value and that it is true. When I first heard of the new "planet" Chiron, which is now designated a comet, I thought, "Oh no! Just another squiggle to add to the already confusing array of items in a chart to synthesize and interpret." At first, hoping it would go away, I ignored it, as I had previously ignored the asteroids, the transplutonian planets, invisible planets and other assorted "points" and "parts." Not that I don't find many of these significant. I do. I'm fully convinced that every speck of dust "out there" probably has a significance for those on earth. Doesn't even the Bible imply as much when it says the very hairs on our head are numbered? Yet, unless one has the mind of an advanced computer, it is best to just consider the major "specks" or risk becoming hopelessly overwhelmed by the sheer volume of detail.

I continued to ignore Chiron and went on with my personal research in cosmobiology, especially the study of transiting midpoints, something we'll come to in a later chapter. While working on one particular problem, I could find no "astrological" explanation for a series of events. So, curiosity winning out, I ordered a Chiron ephemeris and began a little research. I found that Chiron did seem active at times. There was definitely something worth looking into here. But I

1

did not see enough to indicate the kind of major events I was studying. Next I turned my attention to studying Chiron in midpoint combinations and a door slowly began to open. I have since that time found to my satisfaction that Chiron is indeed a major astrological body, worthy of major study. In fact, I now feel that leaving Chiron out of the horoscope would be akin to leaving out one of the major planets like Uranus or Pluto.

At this time I read all the available literature on Chiron in an attempt to distill a meaning that I could work with on a daily basis. Though the information on Chiron was meager, I do owe a debt of gratitude to those who have already blazed a path for this new planet. I hope this little volume will add to what will soon become an explosion in the field of cosmobiology, and in particular, the study of Chiron, a major body worthy of consideration by astrologers.

What is Chiron?

Chiron was discovered by astronomer Charles Kowal on November 1, 1977. It has an elliptical orbit around the Sun and its cycle runs from between 49 and 51 years. Though it is about the size of an asteroid, Chiron is not in the asteroid belt, which lies in a plane between the orbits of Mars and Jupiter. Instead it orbits between the planets of Saturn and Uranus, swinging sometimes closer to one, sometimes closer to the other. It *is* extremely small in size, but as with Pluto, size can be deceptive.

Many have already been deeply involved in the study of Chiron. Zane Stein, one of the earliest researchers formed a committee for this purpose. There is now a glyph [⚷], an association, and an ephemeris of Chiron. Several tentative ideas have been advanced on the basic meaning of this new stellar body.

In the past astrologers have found that the time in history in which a new planet is discovered has much to do with its subsequent meaning. It is still early in Chiron's discovery history. Perhaps years from now, in retrospect, we will grasp its full significance. For example, the discovery of Uranus in 1781 presaged the industrial revolution as well as revolutions in governments in France and America and elsewhere. It ushered in many new inventions and other discoveries in science and technology which revolutionized society and thrust us headlong into the modern world. Uranus also has a special affinity for electricity, another development which changed modern life. Hence today, key words associated with the meaning and interpretation of Uranus are "shocking," "revolutionary," "novel," and "unexpected." Uranus was an electrical "bolt from the blue." An interesting way of looking at a planet's discovery is to realize that we didn't really "need" Uranus until it was found. Something more than the old standbys, Mars and Saturn was needed to account for auto accidents, modern surgery, electrical activity, and the whole host of modern machinery.

The discovery of Neptune is similar. Most astrologers would agree that Neptune is the hardest planet to write about and to understand. It's supposed to be the planet of illusion, and it certainly is "illusive." We still aren't "precisely" sure about all of the meanings of this planet. Its the nature of Neptune to be vague. Neptune has definite correspondences with fluids, vapors, gasses and waves of every kind, and likewise to their discovery such as radio, television, movies and telephones. Neptune is also related to chemistry and the discovery of new elements. Neptune, the planetary "weirdo" of the group can and usually does signify extremes, being anything from absolute anguish to utter bliss, with no explanations for either.

Pluto, on the other hand, is small but potent. Discovered in 1930, it represents to astrologers nuclear energy, destruction and regeneration. Perhaps the energy of Pluto is so powerful because it is compressed like black holes. Pluto heralded the atomic age which brought great changes for the masses — another keyword for Pluto. When Pluto makes a major aspect to your chart, you know it!

Now we have Chiron, the new "kid on the block." Though not prone to prattle on about rainbow bridges and crystals, too reminiscent of Neptune, I do believe Chiron has something to do with the "new age movement." It appears to signify a turning point in man's history, from which, incidentally, there is no turning back. One door has opened and another must now be shut. Which doors will provide a clue to ultimate meaning of Chiron.

Chiron seems to parallel great advances in biology, especially genetics. It was found to be rising in the chart of the first test-tube

3

baby. Perhaps it stands for the Earth as a test-tube and the birth of a new age. But Chiron represents much more than just biology. I have seen it stand for all the things so far suggested, such as a key, a door, a bridge, a breakthrough, and most of all a turning point. Not just a change either but a point of no return. Something is gone forever but something else takes its place. Chiron is both a key and a door to the future, but also a lock on the past, like the end of childhood when crossing into adolescence. Eventually the meanings of Chiron will be synthesized into a coherent whole.

Whatever Chiron's implications are on a grand scale for mankind, it also has implications in our daily lives. That Chiron does work in the delineation of horoscopes convinced me of this. This body brings turning points and transitions to our mundane lives as well as signifying major things for mankind as a whole, just like Uranus, Neptune and Pluto have been doing. As each of these outer planets meant a change from one era of history to another, so Chiron must represent another transition for man. The Star of Bethlehem is often thought to have signaled the beginning of the Piscean era: Chiron may well herald the true Age of Aquarius.

Breakthrough

A real breakthrough for me with this new body came while observing transits in the chart of a friend. This person, Mr. J., experienced three important events in the same month relating to his family, notably three of his four children. There was very little in his chart by direction or transit to account for these kinds of events and I knew from experience that there should be "something" astrological representing these experiences. There is **always** a correlation in the transits to one's chart when physical or psychological changes are perceived in consciousness as affecting one's life.

During that month, Mr. J helped his son buy his first car, signaling a new lifestyle for his son not to mention the new worries for himself! About a week later another son had a near brush with the law causing worries for Mr. J. and a changed relationship with this son. Finally toward the end of the month a daughter experienced a major upheaval in her life causing excitement which upset the whole family including

4

Mr. J. All three of these events had a similar theme, that of a turning point or transition, in a man's relationship with the members of his family.

Now many would suggest explaining these events using perhaps large orbs of outer planets to some factor in Mr. J.'s chart or using directions that are six months past or present. In my work I have found orbs unnecessary and I have also found directions to be much more exact than this. Time and again I have found transits signaling events to be exact and to pertain to the meanings of the planets and points involved. This is the beauty and science of using midpoints — everything fits. For this reason understanding midpoints will be crucial in studying Chiron and a chapter is devoted to explaining this topic. Briefly for now, a midpoint is any point equidistant between any two points or planets in a horoscope. I combined Chiron with Mr. J.'s personal planets and points to see if I had missed an important mid-point in his chart. Having no luck with this approach I experimented further by investigating the transiting midpoints to Mr. J.'s chart. This is the same idea as midpoints in a chart except that these points are equidistant between any two transiting planets. Not finding anything spectacular, I used the Chiron ephemeris to locate the position of Chiron that month. Then I located the transiting midpoint between Chiron and each of the outer planets. I had found a key.

PL/CH = A

No this isn't algebra, though it is like a formula. This combination t(PL/CH) represents a transiting midpoint between Pluto and Chiron and the equal sign means it contacted Mr. J.'s Ascendant during the month under consideration. During that month, Pluto was retrograde; Chiron was retrograde and slowing, and it became stationary and then slowly turned direct. Because of the motions of Pluto and Chiron the midpoint between them was the same on three different days of the month. The exact midpoint between Pluto in Scorpio and Chiron in Cancer was 8 Virgo 11. This was the exact sign and degree of Mr. J.'s Ascendant!

To check further lets use some key words for each of the planets in-volved and see if the resulting combination fits the events observed.

5

Pluto   - major, fated, intense, powerful
Chiron   - turning point, transition
Ascendant - family, environment

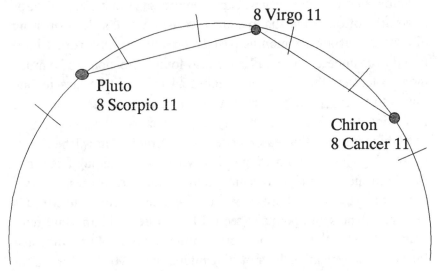

8 Virgo 11

Pluto
8 Scorpio 11

Chiron
8 Cancer 11

Figure 1. Midpoint Between Chiron in Cancer and Pluto in
        Scorpio.

We have a major turning point involving members of one's family.
This certainly does seem to correlate well with Mr. J.'s experiences
during that fated month.

Of course, conclusions can never be based on any one event or
experience but must instead be substantiated over and over again to be
useful and valid. Feeling sure I had found a key to the meaning of
Chiron. I set out on a path that led ultimately to the writing of this
book. For several years I combed through data, checking and re-
checking and learning along the way how Chiron combined in influence with the planets. To my satisfaction I have found that Chiron
works — and that it works in ways that can be shown, measured and
proven. I've also found that Chiron is especially active in events m-
arking key turning points in life. Chiron not only opened doors to a
deeper understanding of the horoscope, but showed me time and time
again the importance of using midpoints. It also taught me that these

transiting midpoints are so accurate for certain events that they can even be used to rectify charts.

But to fully test Chiron in its influence we have to combine it in a multitude of ways over a multitude of years. If Chiron is a major new astrological body of importance, it will stand the test of time and will prove itself in practice. For me, it was in using Chiron with midpoints in the chart, by transit and by direction, that the truth and meanings of this little body began to unfold. The study of Chiron and midpoints should be combined for in practice they are inseparable. In fact, Chiron seems to act as a catalyst, another proffered meaning, bringing out the full potential of each of the planets and personal points. Chiron, also called a teacher, has been my tutor in this work, closing old doors and opening new ones. Is this the last major body in the Solar System to be discovered? Or is it the job of Chiron to finally bring everything together and increase our understanding of the whole? There is so much yet to be learned but now at least we have a key to a deeper insight into our lives.

2

Midpoints – Their Time Has Come

"He counts the stars and calls them by name."
Psalms 147:4

Midpoints

Midpoints are the core and essence of cosmobiology. Although the concept is not new, it has not been studied in great detail until this century. However even the ancients knew of midpoints. They often recognized the importance of the place situated exactly between planets or points. There is an old well-known configuration often seen in the natal chart called a Yod. It is sometimes known as the "Finger of God," because it seemed to be of fated significance. The Yod is formed when two planets are sextile (60°) to each other and both in quincunx (150°) to a third planet.

In Figure 2, Mercury is quincunx both the Moon and Venus and is also indirectly at the midpoint between the two planets. There is also often seen another configuration in the natal chart called a T-Square (Figure 3). Here, two planets are opposite each other and a third planet is square to both. The planet that is square to both is also indirectly at their midpoint.

Over the years astrologers such as Guido Bonati, Alan Leo and others were aware of the importance of midpoints. Alfred Witte, famous for his contribution to the Hamburg School of Astrology, also used midpoints, which he called half-sums, in forming his "planetary pictures." But it was not until this century, and the work of Reinhold Ebertin, that the principle of midpoints was fully explored and brought

9

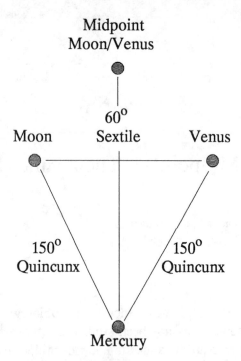

Figure 2. Yod Formation: Mercury at the Midpoint of the Moon and Venus.

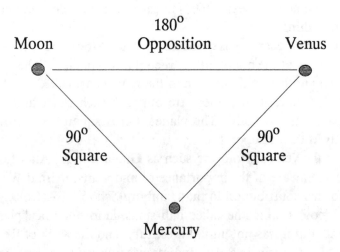

Figure 3. T-Square Formation.

into more frequent use. I have found nearly everything discovered by Ebertin regarding midpoints to be valid in my own experience.

What are Midpoints?

A midpoint is simply a point or place exactly between any two planets (SU, MO, ME, VE, MA, JU, SA, UR, NE, PL, CH) or personal points (M, A, MN). For example if the Sun in a person's chart is at 4 Virgo 02 and Mars is at 19 Virgo 39 then the exact point equidistant between the two would be located at 11 Virgo 50 (Figure 4).

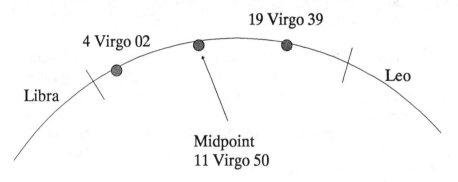

Figure 4. Midpoint Between 4 Virgo 02 and 19 Virgo 39.

This midpoint would be written as SU/MA. The faster planet is always written first, except the Sun which is always first. So a transiting or a natal planet at 11 Virgo 50 would be conjunct the SU/MA midpoint. But other transiting aspects can contact this point indirectly. For example, a planet at 11 Gemini 50 would be square the SU/MA midpoint. A planet at 11 Pisces 50 would be opposite. This type of midpoint is easy to see when looking at a chart. More difficult to see but just as important are planets further apart or in different signs. For example, if the Sun is at 4 Virgo 02 and the Moon is at 8 Capricorn 10, then the exact midpoint between them would be at 6 Scorpio 06 or its opposite at 6 Taurus 06 (Figure 5). We usually refer to the one which is closest.

An easy way to locate these midpoints between planets is with a conversion chart of 360°.

Conversion Chart

Aries	0°- 29°	Libra	180°-209°
Taurus	30°- 59°	Scorpio	210°-239°
Gemini	60°- 89°	Sagittarius	240°-269°
Cancer	90°-119°	Capricorn	270°-299°
Leo	120°-149°	Aquarius	300°-329°
Virgo	150°-179°	Pisces	330°-359°

For example if Jupiter is at 14 Pisces 05 and Uranus is at 25 Libra 00 Libra, convert Jupiter to 344°05'and Uranus to 205°00'. Add them together to get 549°05', and divide this sum by two. This yields 274°33' or 4 Capricorn 33.

So the Jupiter/Uranus (JU/UR) midpoint is at 4 Capricorn 33. There are usually 78 midpoints to consider, 13 more if you include Chiron — and you should! You can go through this procedure to locate any midpoint either in a chart or in transit. But it is much easier nowadays to send for computerized midpoint printouts of all the points and planets in a natal chart. Many companies offer this service saving hours of computation time. Table I shows just such a printout listing the midpoints arranged in planetary sequence with the individual planets listed first. In this example from ACS Services, Inc.,[1] the glyphs are used to represent each planet.

When these midpoints are activated by transits or directions, the results will be apparent. You know pretty much what kinds of events to expect when a major planet transits the Sun or Mars in a natal chart. You will also find an event when, for example, a planet transits the natal midpoint SU/MA. The combination of the three factors makes for a very clear picture in chart interpretation.

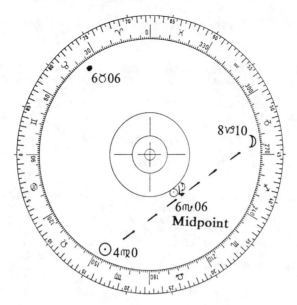

Figure 5. Midpoint between planets in different signs on a 360° dial.

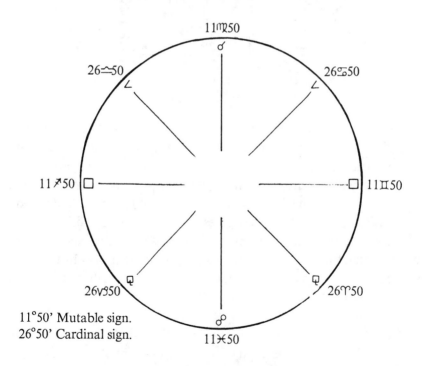

11°50' Mutable sign.
26°50' Cardinal sign.

Figure 6. Angular Relationships -- 360° dial.

13

TABLE I. Midpoints Arranged in Planetary Sequence

☉	04♍02	♇	05♎27	☉/♃	09♊03	☽/☿	11♏01	☽/M	03♏34
☽	08♑15	A	18♏45	/♄	09♌41	/♀	26♎54	/☊	27♐17
☿	13♍47	M	28♌52	/♅	29♍31	/♂	13♏57	/⚷	01♓11
♀	15♌33	☊	16♐19	/♆	20♎27	/♃	11♒10	☿/♀	29♌40
♂	19♍40	⚷	24♈07	/♇	19♍45	/♄	11♎48	/♂	16♍43
♃	14♓05	☉/☽	06♏09	/A	11♎24	/♅	01♐38	/♃	13♊56
♄	15♋20	/☿	08♍54	/M	01♍27	/♆	22♐34	/♄	14♌33
♅	25♎00	/♀	24♌48	/☊	25♎11	/♇	21♏51	/♅	04♎24
♆	06♐52	/♂	11♍51	/⚷	29♊04	/A	13♐30	/♆	25♎19

☿/♇	24♍37	♀/♆	11♎13	♂/♆	28♎16	♃/♇	24♐46
/A	16♎16	/♇	10♍30	/♇	27♍33	/A	16♑25
/M	06♍19	/A	02♎09	/A	19♎12	/M	06♊28
/☊	00♏03	/M	22♌13	/M	09♍16	/☊	00♒12
/⚷	03♋57	/☊	15♎56	/☊	02♏59	/⚷	04♈06
♀/♂	02♍36	/⚷	19♊50	/⚷	06♋53	♄/♅	05♍10
/♃	29♉49	♂/♃	16♐52	♃/♄	14♉42	/♆	26♍06
/♄	00♌26	/♄	17♌30	/♅	04♑32	/♇	25♌24
/♅	20♍17	/♅	07♎20	/♆	25♑28	/A	17♍02

♄/M	07♌06	♆/♇	06♏10	A/M	08♎49
/☊	00♎50	/A	27♏49	/☊	02♐32
/⚷	04♊43	/M	17♎52	/⚷	06♒26
♅/♆	15♏56	/☊	11♐36	M/☊	22♎36
/♇	15♎14	/⚷	15♒29	/⚷	26♊29
/A	06♏53	♇/A	27♎06	☊/⚷	20♒13
/M	26♍56	/M	17♍10		
/☊	20♏40	/☊	10♏53		
/⚷	24♑33	/⚷	14♋47		

Midpoints may help explain some of the confusion regarding orbs. Many times in the past astrologers may have explained an event in terms of a transit of an outer planet, say to the Sun. Since the event did not occur when the transit was exact, they would say the event occurred when the transit was within, say, a few degrees of the Sun. Some used orbs of influence as wide as 15 degrees. In my own work with transits I have found orbs to be unnecessary. When using midpoints, transits are most often found to be **exact.** So instead of the transit hitting the Sun, it may have been contacting the SU/MA or some other midpoint.

Angles

The other extremely important discovery made by Ebertin in his work was the importance of the hard angles in relation to events. Ebertin found the old "good" angles such as trines and sextiles to be vaguely representative of conditions. It was, he said, the angles divisible by 45 degrees, the old "hard" angles, that were the most important indicators of **events**. Whether these aspects were good or bad, positive or negative, depended entirely on the **combination** of the planets and points involved, rather than the kind of aspect made. He found that the most important aspects corresponding to events were the conjunction, the square, the opposition, the semisquare, and the sesquiquadrate. Others have agreed that these angles of 0°, 90°, 180°, 45°, and 135° are the most significant indicators of events.

Taking our previous example of the SU/MA midpoint at 11 Virgo 50 (Figure 6):

The square would be 11 Gemini 50 or 11 Sagittarius 50.

The opposition 11 Pisces 50

The semisquare 26 Cancer 50 or 26 Libra 50.

The sesquiquadrate 26 Aries 50 or 26 Capricorn 50

In cosmobiology all of the 45° angles are equally important. So if the SU/MA midpoint is 11 Virgo 50 then a planet at any of the above angles would be equally powerful in effect. The only exception might be the conjunction which is the most potent of aspects. In his work Ebertin developed a useful tool called the 90° dial (Figure 7). On this dial all the natal planets and points can be arranged around a circle of 90° starting at 0° Cancer. This groups together all the factors from the same quadruplicities. So the cardinal signs are shown from 0° to 30°, the fixed signs from 30° to 60°, and the mutable signs from 60° to 90°.

Immediately apparent is that all the squares, opposition and conjunctions are listed in the same place and their semisquares and sesquiquadrates are exactly opposite on the dial. This method eliminates the house system almost entirely. The 90° dial is especially useful in studying directions of solar arc. Once you have listed all the natal factors on both circles of the dial all you have to do is rotate one of the dials the amount of the solar arc accrued to a particular date and you have a complete direction picture. Midpoints also come listed for the 90° dial which greatly facilitates this work. Table II shows a printout with the midpoints arranged in the 90° sequence as they would appear on the 90° dial.

There are many publications available on this method. Both Eleonora Kimmel's *Fundamentals of Cosmobiology*[2] and Reinhold Ebertin's *Applied Cosmobiology*[3] present excellent discussions on the use of the 90° dial. Before leaving this topic there is one more midpoint printout sequence we should mention — the 45° sequence (Table III). Originally Ebertin used this arrangement for a 45° ephemerides to study annual transit patterns. It is extremely useful because it groups all the important angles together including the 45° and the 135° angles. For transit and direction work this is ideal, as the semisquare and the sesquiquadrate aspects are so easily overlooked.

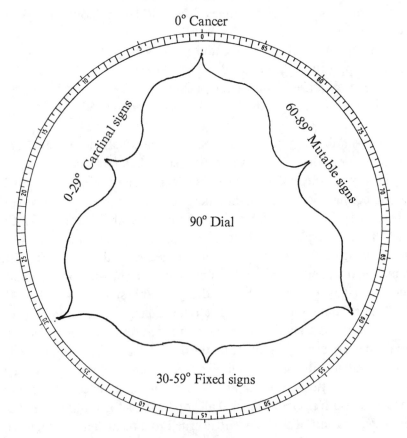

Figure 7. The 90-Degree Dial.

Taking an example from this chart we see the midpoint JU/NE at 25° 28' of a cardinal sign and the midpoint ME/NE which is also in a cardinal sign at 25° 19'. What you also see in the same location is the midpoint VE/PL which is at 10° 30' of a mutable sign, but on the 45°

16

Table II and III

MIDPOINTS ARRANGED IN 90° SEQUENCE

♄/☊ 00 50	☽ 08 15	☿/A 16 16	☉/☊ 25 11	♂/☊ 32 59
♀/A 02 09	A/M 08 49	♃/A 16 25	☿/♆ 25 19	☽/M 33 34
☿/⚷ 03 57	♀/♆ 11 13	♆/M 17 52	♃/♆ 25 28	☉/☽ 36 09
♃/⚷ 04 06	☉/A 11 24	♂/A 19 12	☽/♀ 26 54	♆/♇ 36 10
☿/♅ 04 24	☽/♄ 11 48	☉/♆ 20 27	♇/A 27 06	A/⚷ 36 26
♃/♅ 04 32	♇/⚷ 14 47	M/☊ 22 36	♂/♆ 28 16	♅/A 36 53
♇ 05 27	♅/♇ 15 14	⚷ 24 07	☿/☊ 30 03	♄/M 37 06
♂/⚷ 06 53	♄ 15 20	♅/⚷ 24 33	♃/☊ 30 12	☉/♄ 39 41
♂/♅ 07 20	♀/☊ 15 56	♅ 25 00	♀/♄ 30 26	♇/☊ 40 53

☽/☿ 41 01	A 48 45	☿/♀ 59 40	♄/♅ 65 10
☽/♃ 41 10	☊/⚷ 50 13	♀/♃ 59 49	☿/M 66 19
☽/♂ 43 57	♅/☊ 50 40	☽/⚷ 61 11	♃/M 66 28
☿/♄ 44 33	☽/♇ 51 51	☉/M 61 27	♆ 66 52
♃/♄ 44 42	♀/M 52 13	☽/♅ 61 38	☉/☿ 68 54
♆/⚷ 45 29	☉/♀ 54 48	A/☊ 62 32	☉/♃ 69 03
♀ 45 33	♄/♇ 55 24	♀/♂ 62 36	♂/M 69 16
♅/♆ 45 56	♆/A 57 49	☉ 64 02	♀/♇ 70 30
♂/♄ 47 30	M 58 52	♄/⚷ 64 43	♆/☊ 71 36

☉/♂ 71 51	♇/M 77 10	M/⚷ 86 29
☽/A 73 30	♂ 79 40	♅/M 86 56
☿ 73 47	☉/♇ 79 45	☽/☊ 87 17
☿/♃ 73 56	♀/⚷ 79 50	♂/♇ 87 33
♃ 74 05	♀/♅ 80 17	☉/⚷ 89 04
☊ 76 19	☽/♆ 82 34	☉/♅ 89 31
☿/♂ 76 43	☿/♇ 84 37	
♂/♃ 76 52	♃/♇ 84 46	
♄/A 77 02	♄/♆ 86 06	

MIDPOINTS ARRANGED IN 45° SEQUENCE

/⚷ 00 29	☿/♅ 04 24	☽ 08 15	☿/♀ 14 40	☉/M 16 27
♀ 00 33	♃/♅ 04 32	A/M 08 49	♇/⚷ 14 47	☽/♅ 16 38
/☊ 00 50	☊/⚷ 05 13	☉/♀ 09 48	♀/♃ 14 49	A/☊ 17 32
/♆ 00 56	♇ 05 27	♄/♇ 10 24	♅/♇ 15 14	♀/♂ 17 36
/A 02 09	♅/☊ 05 40	♀/♆ 11 13	♄ 15 20	♆/M 17 52
/♄ 02 30	☽/♇ 06 51	☉/A 11 24	♀/☊ 15 56	☉ 19 02
A 03 45	♂/⚷ 06 53	☽/♄ 11 48	☽/⚷ 16 11	♂/A 19 12
/⚷ 03 57	♀/M 07 13	♆/A 12 49	☿/A 16 16	♄/⚷ 19 43
/⚷ 04 06	♂/♅ 07 20	M 13 52	♃/A 16 25	♄/♅ 20 10

☉/♆ 20 27	♅/⚷ 24 33	♇/A 27 06	☊ 31 19
☿/M 21 19	♅ 25 00	♂/♆ 28 16	☿/♂ 31 43
♃/M 21 28	☉/☊ 25 11	☽/A 28 30	♂/♃ 31 52
♆ 21 52	☿/♆ 25 19	☿ 28 47	♄/A 32 02
M/☊ 22 36	♃/♆ 25 28	☿/♃ 28 56	♇/M 32 10
☉/☿ 23 54	♀/♇ 25 30	♃ 29 05	♂/☊ 32 59
☉/♃ 24 03	♆/☊ 26 36	☿/☊ 30 03	☽/M 33 34
⚷ 24 07	☉/♂ 26 51	♃/☊ 30 12	♂ 34 40
♂/M 24 16	☽/♀ 26 54	♀/♄ 30 26	☉/♇ 34 45

♀/⚷ 34 50	☉/♄ 39 41	♂/♇ 42 33
♀/♅ 35 17	♃/♇ 39 46	☽/♂ 43 57
☉/☽ 36 09	♇/☊ 40 53	☉/⚷ 44 04
♆/♇ 36 10	☽/☿ 41 01	☉/♅ 44 31
A/⚷ 36 26	♄/♆ 41 06	☿/♄ 44 33
♅/A 36 53	☽/♃ 41 10	♃/♄ 44 42
♄/M 37 06	M/⚷ 41 29	
☽/♆ 37 34	♅/M 41 56	
☿/♇ 39 37	☽/☊ 42 17	

printout would be shown as 25° 30' of a cardinal sign, its semisquares and sesquiquadrates. It takes a little time to get used to looking at midpoints arranged in a 45° sequence but these minor angles are too important to overlook. The 45° sequence is invaluable for locating quickly these 45° and 135° angles in the natal chart.

It is standard procedure when using midpoints to use the equal (=) sign to relate these aspects since they are all equally effective. Thus, in the midpoint structure, (Uranus)$_t$ = SU/MA, Uranus is 0°, 45°, 90°, 135°, or 180° of SU/MA. The combination of these three planetary factors gives an interpretation that is much more precise. Of UR = SU/MA the CSI[4] says:

> ...*premature action or hastiness, impulsive behavior, the tendency to do one's work in a state of excitement, the overtaxing of one's strength. Sudden events or adjustment to new circumstances.*

Midpoint Structures

Although this volume will not go into great detail on this topic, it is well for the reader to be familiar with them. Midpoint structures are a means of studying or reading the whole chart to understand patterns of character and destiny. Under each planet and point in a native's chart are listed the main midpoints which contact them by hard aspect. Usually a distance or "orb" of influence is about 2 degrees for the Sun, Midheaven and Ascendant and 1½ degree for the rest of the factors. So, for example, if Venus is 15° 33' of a fixed sign then any midpoint 1½° on either side of 15° 33' fixed sign would be listed under Venus. For example, we see that under Venus (Table IV) is listed the midpoint SU/UR which is 1° 02' from Venus by semisquare.

These midpoint structures give a clear picture of character and events held in the natal chart waiting to be triggered by transits and directions.

Signatures

Over the years cosmobiologists have discovered many midpoint combinations in the natal chart and many transiting combinations of planets that seem to have a signature or nickname. For example, the SA/NE midpoint is commonly known as the "illness axis" because it is so often

Table IV

NATAL CHART
45° ASPECTS, 2° ORBS FOR ☉, ☽, ASC AND MC,
1° 30' ORBS FOR THE OTHERS.

NUMBERS ARE THE MIDPOINT ASPECT ORBS IN ° AND

☉	☽	☿	♀	♂
1 26	1 32	0 17	1 02	1 29
♀—☌—♂	☉—⚼—♀	☽—□—A	☉—∠—♅	☉—∠—☽
0|10	1|03	0|31	1|29	0|05
♂—∠—A	♀—⚼—M	♂—∠—♆	☉—∠—⚷	☉—☌—♇
1|08	0|55	1|25	0|60	1|06
♄—☌—♅	♂—□—♅	♃—⚼—☊	☿—☌—♄	☽—∠—M
0|41	1|22		0|51	0|37
♄—□—⚷	♂—☍—⚷		♃—□—♄	♀—☌—♅
1|10	0|33		0|16	0|10
♆—∠—M	A—□—M		♄—∠—☊	♀—□—⚷
1|30			0|23	
A—□—☊			♅—∠—♆	
			0|04	
			♆—☍—⚷	

♃	♄	♅	♆	♇
0 34	1 07	1 06	0 33	1 04
☽—□—A	☉—∠—M	☉—∠—☿	☿—□—M	☿—☌—♅
0|58	1|18	0|57	0|24	1|26
☿—⚼—☊	☽—⚼—♅	☉—⚼—♃	♃—☍—M	♂—□—⚷
1|22	0|51	0|10	0|44	0|55
♀—⚼—♄	☽—⚼—⚷	☉—☌—☊	M—∠—☊	♃—□—♅
0|49	0|40	0|19		1|22
♂—⚼—♆	☿—∠—♀	☿—□—♆		♃—☍—⚷
	0|56	0|30		0|12
	☿—□—A	♀—∠—♇		♅—∠—☊
	0|31	0|44		0|14
	♀—∠—♃	♂—∠—M		☊—⚼—⚷
	0|36	0|28		
	♀—□—☊	♃—□—♆		
	1|05			
	♃—☍—A			
	0|06			
	♅—□—♇			
	0|33			
	♇—☌—⚷			

A	M	☊	⚷
0 38	0 48	0 24	0 12
☿—∠—♅	☿—☌—♀	☿—□—♂	☉—⚼—☿
0|12	0|57	0|53	0|03
☿—⚼—⚷	♀—□—♃	♀—□—♄	☉—∠—♃
1|15	1|22	0|33	1|04
♂—□—♄	♅—∠—♇	♂—☌—♃	☉—□—☊
0|47	1|04	0|43	1|13
♃—∠—♅	♆—□—A	♄—□—A	☿—☍—♆
0|21	0|55	0|50	1|24
♃—⚼—⚷	♇—∠—⚷	♇—□—M	♀—⚼—♇
1|55			0|09
♅—☌—☊			♂—∠—M
1|28			1|22
☊—□—⚷			♃—□—♆

present in cases of disease. For similar reasons MA/SA is known as the "death axis," though it often just signifies physical hardship. The MA/UR midpoint is known as the injury or accident axis. The JU/UR midpoint is so positive in manifestation that it is often called the "thank the Lord" aspect. There are signatures in natal chart midpoint structures that can indicate particular careers. JU = SU/ME, for example, is often found in the charts of physicians, and means "the good doctor." Some combinations in the chart are indicative of certain diseases *if other factors predispose.* The combination of Pluto, Saturn and Venus can suggest diabetes. It doesn't seem to matter either if the combination is found as PL = VE/SA, VE = SA/PL or SA = VE/PL. All of the ramifications have not yet been worked out, but there is enough evidence to suggest a need for future study.

Ebertin's CSI is a good place to start in gathering information about various midpoint combination meanings. You may even discover some of your own. Listed below are a few combinations that have developed signatures over the years. There are, however, many more.

MA/NE	infectious disease
VE/JU	popularity
MO/PL	schizophrenia
SU/SA	crises or illness
SU/NE/PL	polio and blood diseases
MA/SA/PL	suicide or assault
SA/PL/MN	adult cancer
SU/ME/UR	orators
MA/JU/NE	chemists
SU/MA/PL	atomic scientists
SU/SA/M	brain tumors
JU/NE/PL	the gambler
ME/UR/NE	epilepsy
MO/NE/PL	alcoholics
VE/UR/JU/PL	musical ability

Aspects

With midpoints we have been looking at the main "hard" angles as aspects indicating events. There are some other aspects not previously considered that may be significant. Zane Stein[5] notes that the 165° aspect seems to correlate with Chiron in some way. I too have noticed this. I have also observed the 22½° aspect having effect from time to time. It may well turn out that each of the heavenly bodies has an affinity for a particular aspect and that it is much stronger in one particular position.

The former good aspects like the trine and the sextile have not disappeared entirely from the scene, but their influence is more subtle. These aspects are often viewed as a protective influence hovering in the background rather than fighting in the main arena. The hard aspects symbolize actions brought to our consciousness. They are easier to grasp and see because they correlate so well with events. But while studying events it can be important to note the presence of the softer aspects as they can have a mitigating effect on the "bad guys." One example: A young family had a child who was seriously ill, on the brink of death itself. A whole trail of negative directions and transits dodged the charts of both the parents and the child. However, at that time, the mother had Pluto stationary trining her natal Venus (loved ones) exactly. This would seem to prognosticate a happy outcome and indeed it did as the child fully recovered. The softer aspects do not seem to have much importance in relation to the midpoints. It is almost as if there are two different systems operating side by side and not necessarily interacting.

Directions

In a later chapter we will examine these matters in more detail but here it suffices to point out that including midpoints when directing a chart completely broadens the entire field of prognostication. Now, in addition to checking the ten major planetary indicators in a progressed or directed chart, using the midpoints will cover a whole year with contacts occurring monthly and even weekly. We'll take an example here to show how this can work.

A young man was 16 years old in September and his solar arc of direction was 15° 30'. In May, 9 months later, the solar arc directions were as follows:

Solar Arc $\quad$ 16° 15' $JU_s = MO$
$\qquad\qquad$ 16° 19' $PL_s = MN/M$
$\qquad\qquad$ 16° 19' $CH_s = UR/M$

During the first part of the month when directed Jupiter contacted the Moon, the interpretation would be a love contact, and indeed, he did develop a relationship with a new girlfriend. The directions at the end of the month (according to the CSI) for PLs = MN/M indicate success with others. My own interpretation for CHs = UR/M would indicate that a turning point or breakthrough in career, a success, would be imminent. What did happen? This young man with his partner won a National Debating Contest. There were corresponding transits as well and transiting Jupiter on the day of the event semisquared his Midheaven, effectively triggering the directions. Using midpoints in directing a chart gives a clearer picture of coming events. Just a few examples involving Chiron:

$MA_s = MN/CH$ woman's brother wins an election
$JU_s = JU/CH$ winning a part in a play
$CH_s = MA/SA$ serious quarrel with a friend
$(ME/CH)_s = SU$ surprising news from a male friend

These directions also serve to show that Chiron works in a directed chart just like the other outer planets and is indeed a **major** astrological body. Now we need to take a closer look at the effect of transits.

Endnotes:

1. ACS Services, Inc., P.O. Box 16430, San Diego, CA 92116.
2. Eleonora Kimmel, *Fundamentals of Cosmobiology* (Tempe: American Federation of Astrologers, 1979).
3. Reinhold Ebertin, *Applied Cosmobiology* (Tempe: American Federation of Astrologers, 1972).
4. Reinhold Ebertin, *The Combination of Stellar Influences*, trans. Dr. Alfred G. Roosedale and Linda Kratzch (7080 Aalen, Germany; Ebertin-Verlag, 1940) available from The American Federation of Astrologers.
5. Zane B. Stein, *Essence and Application - A View From Chiron* (New York: CAO Times, 1988), p.185.

By Transit and Direction

"God's Laws Are Perfect..."
Psalms 19:7

Place of Transits

So many times transits are either over or underestimated in importance. It is best in looking at them to gain some perspective on their place in the cosmic scheme of things. In this way we hope to avoid going to the extremes of practically ignoring them or putting too much emphasis on them and forgetting the whole picture. For example, compare a transit of Saturn to Mars. Unless triggering a direction, a **transit** of Saturn to Mars generally means a hard day, often a physically hard day. Curiously this particular transit often coincides with a visit to the dentist! On the other hand a **direction** of Saturn to Mars is not a daily event but a life event, which could be anything from a major illness or bereavement to a physical fight with serious consequences. Directions affect you consciously for more than one day, even if the triggering event is a one-day occurrence.

Noel Tyl suggested that directions and progressions are like the hour hand on a clock signifying major life themes. In this scheme the transits act as minute hands working out the main themes on a daily basis. In fact, we could further say that the minor transits of the inner planets as well as the asteroids and lesser bodies are like the second hand sweeping daily through our lives, ticking off all the little incidents, events and emotions of daily living that make life interesting. The patterns of destiny and character are written in the clock (the natal chart) or in cosmobiology (the cosmogram). They are worked out through the intermingling of directions and transits throughout our lives. They do not determine destiny by themselves as there are many other considerations in life such as heredity, environment and constitution. But they do contribute their part.

The transits and directions are just signs for us and they obviously follow laws. The Book of Job in the Bible is purported by some to be the oldest written. Listen to God speak to Job from the whirlwind...

"Can you hold back the stars? Can you restrain Orion or Pleiades? Can you ensure the proper sequence of the seasons, or guide the constellation of the Bear with her satellites across the heavens? Do you know the laws of the universe and how the heavens influence the earth?"

Job 38:31-34

Man has his free will to be worked out within the context of these laws. The transits indicate the daily rhythms of life. But I have found the transits of the outer planets to signify daily events of importance to the directions; and when several occur at once they may be just as powerful.

Timing

There are several phenomena it is well to be aware of regarding transits. The first involves the frequent retrograde motion, especially of the outer planets. A planet starts with a direct or forward motion, then apparently stands still, then appears to turn backward, but it is an **apparent** motion as viewed from the earth. Due to this retrograde motion, the planets will often contact the same point in a chart, the same degree, two or three times. Actually each contact will signal an event though it may not appear each time to be of the same intensity. Sometimes one of the two or three contacts appears as a very powerful transit indeed, which makes the other contacts pale by comparison. First, if there is a direction due with a similar meaning or if the transiting planet touches by aspect one of the factors in a current direction then this will probably trigger a major event. There is a second situation in which an outer planet's transit is as potent as a direction, even when no directions or progressions are operating at the time. In this case, the outer planet contacts a point in the chart on the same day as an inner planet, more often the Sun, but occasionally Mars, Mercury or Venus, by an angle of 0°, 45°, 90°, 135°, or 180°. This is very powerful in effect and for good or bad it will partake of the nature of the planets and points involved. A few examples follow in which these transits occurred when no directions were in operation.

PL_t and SU_t = VE/M   a woman meets future mate
UR_t and SU_t = MO/VE   a young man introduced to future girlfriend
UR_t and SU_t = SU   auto accident
CH_t and SU_t = SU/PL   winning a position of leadership

Chiron Transits

Transits of Chiron operate just like those of the outer planets. These daily transits represent events of significance. For example, when Chiron transits the Moon, Venus or the MO/VE midpoint, the event expected is concerned with some minor turning point or breakthrough regarding women, art, love or the emotions — the usual meanings associated with these planets. Chiron also can serve as a triggering factor for the exact day of an event. As with the outer planets, with Chiron there are two exceptions — times when Chiron events will be much more potent. The first, when it triggers a major direction or contacts a sensitive point in a chart by transit on the same day that the Sun does likewise. Secondly, when Chiron is stationary on the same degree which can last anywhere from a few days to a month. If it then aspects a factor in the natal chart, this will signify a major turning point in life relating to whichever planets or points it aspects. One interesting thing about Chiron which differs from the action of the other outer bodies when stationary and transiting a sensitive point in a chart is that, no matter what other factors it touches, there is usually something about a relationship associated with it. In fact this particular kind of transit often signifies a new contact of some sort or a new person in your life.

Keywords

A help in interpreting transits is a list of keywords associated with each planet and point. This gives a broad interpretation at a glance and allows you to immediately incorporate the transit or aspect being considered into the whole picture. The following list is by no means inclusive but serves as a quick reference. Using other sources and your own experience you will become adept at getting the gist of the meaning of a transit at a glance. Remember, too, that all transits have to be considered from the standpoint of the larger picture, which includes the natal chart and its directions. Even clearer portraits emerge with the use of midpoints.

Sun	- male principle, health, body, self, vitality
Moon	- female principle, health, nutrition, children, emotions
Mercury	- communication, news, intellect, young people
Venus	- love, art, rhythm, loved ones and females in general
Mars	- action, energy, males in general
Jupiter	- good fortune, success, happiness
Saturn	- restriction, difficulty, the elderly
Uranus	- sudden, unexpected, novel
Neptune	- illusive, strange, unusual, deceptive
Pluto	- major, fated, intense, the masses
Chiron	- transitions, turning points, breakthroughs
Nodes	- families, groups, ties, associations
Midheaven	- ego, soul, career, success, ones children
Ascendant	- environment, family

Decisions

Chiron's designation as a turning point in life plays a key role in the making of decisions. Each day, you open or close doors based on decisions you make. Chiron does not make the decision. You do. What Chiron does is offer a sign indicating that you have a decision to make regarding something which will be a turning point in some way, no matter how insignificant it may seem. Do you make an appointment for one day or another? Do you go out to dinner or stay home? Though somewhat simplistic, these examples show how even on a daily basis decisions are constantly being made for good or ill which will affect the future in some way. Chiron on a daily basis also indicates where you will find a common ground (another suggested keyword) with others and come to some decision or agreement. In contrast to in the natal chart or cosmogram, Chiron tends to show where and how you will have to make major decisions that will effect a turning point in your life. Chiron also shows where a major breakthrough in life is to occur either in your understanding or in your work. A careful consideration of the active midpoints, in addition to the individual factors in the chart in relation to Chiron, indicates areas that will be touched by these decisions.

A brief look at some examples of Chiron's transits in daily action follows which will give insight into how this body works. Later we will look at some of its more powerful astrological influences.

Example: A man meets a woman while under a powerful Pluto transit. Several weeks later while Chiron is stationary on his MA/JU midpoint he asks for a date and she accepts. Here is an obvious example of the action of Chiron while stationary. Incidentally, the MA/JU midpoint is often found in association with engagements, marriage and like events. What is important to remember in what follows is that these Chiron transits form part of a larger network of other transits and directions. These events occurred on the exact day of the Chiron transit mentioned and show how closely Chiron relates to the event at hand even when only acting as a trigger by direction.

CH_t = A day of a move to a new home. (I have seen this several times for moves. In this instance major directions were also involved but notice how Chiron signals the day of a turning point.)

CH_t = MO/JU little brother's birthday party
CH_t = JU/UR receipt of a gift
CH_t = VE/NE sadness over broken date
CH_t = NE/A failing a test

The following set of transits from Chiron occurred on the exact day of the birth of a new child in a family.

27

Mother - CH$_t$ = MO/JU   a woman's joy
Father - CH$_t$ = VE/A   happy environment
Sister - CH$_t$ = ME/MA male sibling (It was a boy!)
Brother - CH$_t$ = A/M   change in life situation

Witness these Chiron aspects on the day of an adoption

Father - CH$_t$ = M
Mother - CH$_t$ = MO

I have seen repeats of these types of Chiron transits seen below.

CH$_t$ = VE/M   birth of a sister
CH$_t$ = ME/SA   loss of an elderly family member
CH$_t$ = SA/NE   loss of an elderly family member
CH$_t$ = JU/M   successful day in career
CH$_t$ = MA   starting a new job, this is very common
CH$_t$ = MA/SA day of hard physical work

Transits To Chiron
    When Chiron transits its own position in the natal chart, its value
is in the cyclical nature of its own orbit. As we may speak of a Saturn
or Uranus return so we can speak of a Chiron return. In the midst of
important directions, CH$_t$ = CH is often the trigger signaling changes
in life relationships. It is common at both births and deaths, even when
there appears to be no connection between the Chiron transit and the
other transits or directions occurring at the same time. When Chiron
transits the place in a chart of one of the outer planets, it is an event
held in common with many others, and is usually not too important.
What is important is the cycle that is coming to a close. These kinds of
transits need to be looked at from a broader perspective. But even here
you will sometimes find Chiron transiting an outer planet in your chart
and notice how the day of the transit indicates the type of occasion.
For example, CH$_t$ = JU for the day of hearing about a new job and
CH$_t$ = UR for a very exciting day.

Directions

Besides acting as a powerful transit trigger, Chiron is an important developer in the unfolding of events in the directed chart or cosmogram. First we should look at what most cosmobiologists mean when speaking of directions. The information given here is for those who may be unfamiliar with some of the techniques.

Progressions are usually assessed by the day for a year method, whereby each day after birth in the ephemeris equates to one year of life. Symbolic directions consist of artificially moving each natal factor ahead each year the same number of degrees or arc, usually a solar arc. Just using the method of one degree for a year will often give a quick overview of future potentials. Many, though, use an arc of direction that is more personal. One type of solar arc progression, the Naibod method, moves all the factors in the chart ahead by the amount of the Sun's daily motion for a year — about 59°08'. This type of arc is used in radix directions. By another type of solar arc the Sun's rate of motion on the day of birth is multiplied by the number of years of life. Finally there is a personal solar arc based on the Sun's actual forward motion which is used by many in progressions. Though all of the systems have validity, it is the latter which is used throughout this work as it yields the most accurate results.

Solar Arc

To use the solar arc, take the position of the Sun on the day of birth from an ephemeris and subtract it from the position of the Sun for the year (age) of direction.

For example: Sun - day of direction - 28° 29' Cancer
Sun - day of birth   - 8° 28' Cancer
Solar arc for age 21   - 20° 01'

Add each factor in the natal chart the amount of degrees of the solar arc, i.e.,

Natal Sun + Solar Arc = Directed Sun
8 Cancer 28 + 20° 01' = 28 Cancer 29
Natal Moon 12 Capricorn 10 + 20° 01' = 2 Leo 11.

Although these are purely symbolic directions, in actual practice they work and there seems to be some justification for it other than just

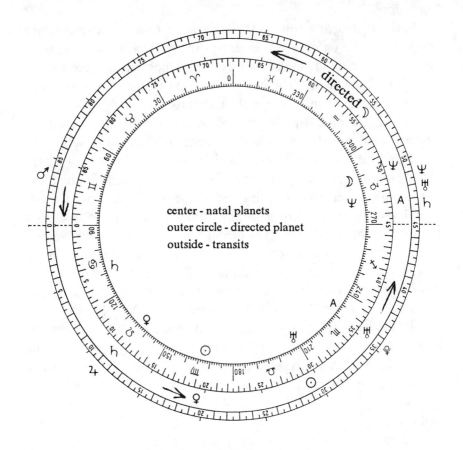

center - natal planets
outer circle - directed planet
outside - transits

Figure 8. Visualizing Directions.

Explosions

Another phenomenon which occurs when using solar arc directions and midpoints, might be called "explosions," for want of a better term. Explosions can occur in a directed chart when one planet or point by direction reaches a midpoint containing itself (Saturn$_s$ = Mercury/Saturn) while at the same time the same midpoint directed reaches one of its components [(Mercury/Saturn)$_s$ = Saturn] or [(Mercury\-Saturn)$_s$ = Mercury]. When this occurs, it causes a veritable "explosion" of contacts in the chart. Ebertin did not place too much emphasis on these types of directions. He suggested basically just following the

the symbolism. They are just as effective as primary directions which required considerable calculation by hand until the advent of the computer. This may well be the true meaning of the "each day will represent one year" (Ezekiel 4:6). Each day here means a solar day. To see this visually, set up a chart with two concentric circles and place the factors from the natal chart in both circles. Then rotate the outer circle counterclockwise by the amount of the solar arc or your "day." In this way the chart is seen as an active moving body. The directed factors activate the natal chart which remains stationary. This also retains the relationships between the natal factors — the core of a person's chart - even in directions. To make it more comprehensive, add the current transits to the picture by placing them around the outermost circle. Figure 8 shows a picture of all the interplay and activity going on in a chart resulting from this method.

Some astrologers who recommend using an oblique ascendant, where the Midheaven is moved ahead by an arc, but the Ascendant instead of being moved in the same manner is taken from a table of houses to correspond to the new Midheaven. Unfortunately this changes the relationship of the natal Midheaven and Ascendant and it is not as effective in actual practice as just directing the natal Ascendant the same number of degrees as the Midheaven. In practice these solar arc directions often work out to the week or even to a day. We can break down the solar arc for a year by advancing the standard by about 5 minutes per month and by about 1 minute for every 6 days.

Transits work like the minute hand on a clock triggering the directions represented by the hour hand. Chiron, transiting, like the outer planets, is a powerful activator of these solar arc directions. Chiron in a transiting midpoint is another potent trigger. This will be discussed in the next chapter. Chiron and the other bodies do not have to touch only a point or planet that is involved in a current direction. The directed position alone of a point or planet making no particular contacts with the natal chart can be stimulated by transits. When this occurs, the natal configurations and structures associated with this planet or point in the natal chart are activated. It happens occasionally that an event is related only to the transiting planet and the directed planet or point it touches.

31

interpretation of the two planets or points involved placing emphasis on whichever planet is predominant. So, for example, if the direction is SU_s = SU/NE, the emphasis would be on the Sun. If the direction is instead NE_s = SU/NE then the emphasis would be on Neptune. Ebertin did not mention the converse midpoint which always occurs at the same time in one of these directions.

These types of directions are much more significant in practice. They are very exciting to work with, and when Chiron is involved in one of them, the results are almost fantastic. Let's take a closer look at one in action and see how it affects what happens in the chart. A young man was elected president of his high school class. The planets involved in the "explosion" in his chart were Venus and Jupiter, ordinarily associated with love of some kind, but in practice often seen to signify popularity, especially with large groups. At the time of the election the directions due were VEs = VE/JU and $(VE/JU)s$ = JU. What in fact happened in the chart is that 14 contacts were occurring all at once! In this example every point and planet is touched by Venus, Jupiter, or a midpoint containing Venus or Jupiter; fourteen planets, personal points or midpoints contact other planets, personal points or midpoints. From many charts observed over several years every explosion occurring in them has been found to represent a major life event. Listed below are the contacts which occurred at the same time with these two directions: VEs = VE/JU and $(VE/JU)s$ = JU.

$(SU/VE)_s$ = SU/JU

$(MO/VE)_s$ = MO/JU

$(ME/VE)_s$ = ME/JU

$(VE/MA)_s$ = MA/JU

VE_s = VE/JU *

$(VE/JU)_s$ = JU *$(VE/SA)s$ = JU/SA

$(VE/UR)_s$ = JU/UR

$(VE/NE)_s$ = JU/NE

$(VE/PL)_s$ = JU/PL

$(VE/CH)_s$ = JU/CH

$(VE/MN)_s$ = JU/MN

$(VE/M)_s$ = JU/M

$(VE/A)_s$ = JU/A

This gives a view of the extent of the chart activation and shows why *explosion* is the word of choice. It is not necessary to direct midpoints to other midpoints on a regular basis. The wealth of detail alone could be confusing. You can observe the really important ones on the 90° dial or just direct them to individual natal factors. Whether there is an explosion or not can be seen when the same two planets or points are in a directed combination, and that tells you that there is also a midpoint with the same combination being directed toward one of the factors. Below are some typical examples observed in people's charts along with the events that occurred simultaneously. No matter which planets and points are involved, the results are always spectacular, for good or for bad, and always associated with the two main factors in the explosion, as shown in the previous example for Venus and Jupiter, denoting popularity.

Example Explosions:

CH_s = CH/M and $(CH/M)_s$ = M   Two major life changes occurring at the same time - a career and a change of residence.

SA_s = MA/SA and $(MA/SA)_s$ = MA serious long-term illness

$(VE/SA)_s$ = VE and SA_s = VE/SA broken engagement

SU_s = SU/PL and $(SU/PL)_s$ = PL attainment of position of leadership in career

MN_s = VE/MN and $(VE/MN)_s$ = VE love affair

MA_s = MA/UR and $(MA/UR)_s$ = UR serious car accident

$(MA/SA)_s$ = A and A_s = MA/SA death of father

This last example is a little different than an explosion. Here we have three factors repeating in the directed configuration. A point and a midpoint are juxtaposed and due as directions at the same time. It is similar in effect to an explosion. It has the flavor of the old idea of mutual rulership of planets in natal charts. This particular case helped to rectify an Ascendant and time of birth.

Triggering the Directed Chart

There is a great deal of confusion as to just how transits trigger the directions. This has not been fully worked out to anyones satisfaction and there are still many conflicting opinions and ideas. Newer technology using computers should be helpful in this endeavor with their ability to keep track of vast amounts of detailed information.

Charles Carter states the Law of Excitation[1], "If at the time that a progressed body is in aspect to another by direction, and either of these bodies form an aspect by transit with either of the two directional bodies, then this transit will excite the direction into immediate operation." I have observed three basic patterns operating and two of them fit this law. Sometimes only one and sometimes all three of these will be operative in a given situation.

In the previous example of the man with directions due of $(MA/SA)_s = A$ and $A_s = MA/SA$, there was a death in the family, notably his father. The transits on the day of the event illustrate two of the three recurrent patterns. In the first pattern, a transit occurs which is similar in meaning to the direction but does not partake of the same factors (points and planets). One of the transits for the day in this case was $NE_t = MO/CH$, signifying an anguishing turning point in relation to the mother and the emotions. Note that although none of the same factors are shown in the current direction, nevertheless the meanings are similar.

The second pattern, which follows Carter's law to some degree was illustrated by a transit of the Sun to the midpoint MA/A. Here the transiting Sun contacted a midpoint which included two of the points involved in the direction, effectively setting it off.

$$SU_t = \underline{MA/A} \quad A_s = \underline{MA}/SA \quad (\underline{MA/SA})_s = \underline{A}$$

Again and again the transiting Sun acts as a main activator of directions, showing its importance in the annual rhythms of daily life and as a timer of events. A similar example is seen in the chart of a woman at the birth of a daughter. The direction due at the time was $M_s = MO$.

34

The transit on the day of birth was CH_t = MO setting off the direction. In another example following the same pattern the direction due was CH_s = JU/PL. A man received approval for an important license he needed for his business. On that day, the midpoint between the transiting Jupiter and Pluto, $(JU/PL)_t$, contacted by conjunction his JU/PL midpoint.

A third but frequently observed pattern that follows Carter's law most closely is when the factors involved in the transit are the same but are juxtaposed from those involved in the direction. For example, in the case of an auto accident the direction was SU_s = UR. The transit on the day of the accident was UR_t = SU. In another case the direction due was MO/UR$_s$ = CH. This was an exciting meeting with a new client. The activating transit on that day was CH_t = MO/UR. It is helpful to keep these three patterns in mind when studying directions and transits. They are, however, not the only triggers to directions. Often some of the lesser transiting midpoints, which we will come to next, and particularly the Moon, can time events to the minute. Now that both directions and transits have been discussed, it cannot be stressed enough how important it is to keep them in proper perspective. A direction of Uranus to MA/SA can be devastating; it might mean a sudden serious illness or even a death. By contrast, a transit of Uranus to MA/SA, unless setting off a direction, probably just means a stressful day. In the case of one young fellow it was a tough physical workout — football tryouts!

Now we shall take a look at a different kind of transit — transiting midpoints — the key to Chiron.

Endnote:
1. Charles Carter, *The Principles of Astrology* (Wheaton, IL: Theosophical Publishing House, 1963), p.160.

4

Transiting Midpoint Keys

"For he has given me the true knowledge of the things that exist to
know the disposition of the whole world and the activity of the elements, the beginning, the end **and the midst of the times,** the movement of the heavens and the changes of seasons, the cycles of the year
and the ordering of the stars."

Wisdom 7:17-18

When we study transiting midpoints things really start coming together. A transiting midpoint is a place equidistant between any two
transiting bodies. These are the hidden transits and without them we
do not have a complete picture of the transits in operation at any given
time. Anyone who has not previously used them and observes them for
a short period of time will be astounded by what they can show. I have
found them more potent acting on their own as transits and in activating directions than any planet by itself. We locate the positions of the
midpoints that are transiting in the same way as we do for a natal
chart. For example, on a given day UR_t is at 9° 45' Capricorn and PL_t
is at 19 Scorpio 25. The midpoint between these two planets is 14
Sagittarius 35.

$$
\begin{aligned}
UR &= 9 \text{ Cap } 45 \quad 279° 45' \\
PL &= 19 \text{ Sco } 25 \ + \ \underline{229° 25'} \\
&\phantom{= 19 \text{ Sco } 25 \ + \ } 508° 70' \\
\text{Divide by 2} &= 254° 35' \ \ 14 \text{ Sagittarius } 35
\end{aligned}
$$

It would be written as $(JU/UR)_t$ = 14 Sag 35. These midpoints give
an even clearer picture of events than a transit of either alone. And

they are exact. To get a quick grasp of the transiting midpoint picture you can compute the midpoints of the major transiting planets on, say, the first and fifteenth of each month. From these it is not too difficult to interpolate for the days in between. I have had to use this method for transiting midpoints involving Chiron as there is no ephemeris for them as yet. For the rest of the transiting midpoints, however, a midpoint ephemeris[1] is available. It lists all the daily transiting midpoint combinations from the Sun through Pluto. The transiting midpoints of the Sun through Mars are not particularly important for this work as they are relatively minor in effect. They are useful in the exact timing of events. One exception applies to some of the transiting Mars midpoints which, when stationary, can resemble a major transit. These often occur with other major directions and transits. You will often see MA/SA in effect on days of other transits that indicate difficulty or hardship. Since this midpoint is known as the "death axis," it can be seen sometimes in effect on the day of a death. MA/UR is often found aspecting a chart on a day of injuries and accidents and MA/NE during times of illness. MA/JU is frequently found in times of success and happiness. But none of these Mars midpoints signal much by themselves. The first transits of import are the Jupiters. Each of the Jupiters in action will now be discussed so as to reveal their meaning and interpretation when aspecting the natal chart or exciting directions.

The Jupiters

The transiting midpoints of JU/SA, JU/UR, JU/NE, JU/PL and JU/MN do not represent earthshaking events, but they do signify a certain good luck, happiness or feeling of joy. It is noted here that JU/MN means either JU and the North or South Node, as it makes no difference in transits whether it is one or the other. The nodes are extremely significant in working with midpoints and their successful application in actual practice validates this. Usually JU/MN means some kind of shared happiness with others such as with family, school or work associates. It often indicates a social occasion such as a party. JU/SA is a more peaceful aspect meaning things are "okay" but not particularly exciting. Transiting JU/NE is an aspect of reverie, reminiscing or anticipation. It's the aspect of daydreaming. JU/UR and JU/PL are the "happiest" of the group and generally always generate some excitement depending on what they are aspecting in a chart. Even when aspecting a hard midpoint in the chart such as SA/NE, they are usually happy aspects even if only indicating happiness in solitude. All the Jupiters have a high correlation in meaning with the midpoint or planet they aspect by transit. The Jupiters, as well as the rest of the transiting midpoints, are frequent activators of solar arc directions. Although pleasantly effective when transiting alone, when they are active at the same time as a more major transit indicating some form of happiness, it will be "a mighty happy day." So, in general, look for daily happenings or feelings with these meanings in mind.

$(JU/SA)_t$ satisfaction or a changing situation
$(JU/NE)_t$ happy feelings
$(JU/UR)_t$ happy surprises
$(JU/PL)_t$ successes
$(JU/MN)_t$ shared happiness

Below are a few examples of these transits in action which should help develop a "feel" for what to expect from them.[*]

$(JU/UR)_t$ = ME   an unexpected letter
$(JU/MN)_t$ = A   hosting a good party
$(JU/NE)_t$ = M   daydreaming about one's good luck
$(JU/PL)_t$ = SU/MN   a brother gets a date for a dance
$(JU/SA)_t$ = VE   noticing a change in attitude in a loved one
$(JU/PL)_t$ = UR/PL   successful completion of a project
$(JU/UR)_t$ = MO/MN   a child brings home good report card

The Saturns

The Saturn midpoint transits are of a class of the more "challenging" aspects often regarded as the "bad guys." Although the thrust of cosmobiology, and indeed most of astrology, is not to look at transits as good or bad; there is no denying that the Saturn transits will not make you feel happy. Even if they signify growth or lead to an eventual improvement of conditions, at the moment of their action their effect will not be perceived as "positive". What is important to remem-

(All the examples in this book are of actual events taken from the lives of real people. None of them have been made up.)

ber is that these are still in the realm of daily events, which are not major, not life deciding. One generally expects Saturn midpoints to be hard, often physically so. Physical exercise my be strenuous but that does not mean it is "bad." Sometimes these transiting aspects mean taking care of things, like preventive medicine.

The SA/UR transiting midpoint best represents irritable tension. And surprisingly this can often be an excitement of a positive nature. It is often seen on days of general happiness but it can indicate nervously awaiting the outcome of something good or bad. Transiting SA/PL is just plain difficult. Picture, for example, a teenage boy trying to get up his courage to call a girl for the first time. This aspect can be hard physically, emotionally or both. SA/NE is truly the worst. Here illness or emotional *angst* is shown. A good description would be depression. SA/MN represents sadness and separation from others. There is such a constant interplay of factors going on in any one person's chart at any given time that it is often difficult to pin down any one particular aspect as being the cause of a particular event. Not that these actually "cause" the events. The examples chosen herein are indicative of situations where there wasn't much else going on in a person's chart. In these cases, the transit description is a surer indication of the event. For example:

$(SA/UR)_t$	= UR	worry over a decision to be made
$(SA/NE)_t$	= A	a minor illness
$(SA/PL)_t$	= VE	saying good bye to a loved one
$(SA/MN)_t$	= A	news of death of a distant relative
$(SA/MN)_t$	= VE/MN	temporary sadness over a separation

The following transiting midpoints involving UR, NE and PL represent daily events also, and are transits of greater significance than the Saturns and Jupiters. They are certainly as powerful as the transit of any of the outer planets and sometimes much more so.
$(UR/PL)_t$

40

The Uranus/Pluto transiting midpoint is a potent and very positive combination even when contacting a difficult midpoint or planet. There is usually an element of surprise and especially joy associated with it.

(UR/MN)$_t$

Similar to JU/MN in effect, it is often a social aspect when aspecting positive factors but it can be difficult if aspecting a difficult point or midpoint. It almost always refers to involvement with groups whether these are friends, family, work or school associates.

(UR/NE)$_t$

Sudden or unexpected is the Uranus component, but like anything involving Neptune there is usually an element of strangeness involved. A good keyword might be "unbelievable." The feeling is, "Wow, is this real?" but it can be very good or very bad depending on what it aspects in the cosmogram and depending on other factors in the transit and direction picture. Sometimes there is a psychic element to it. Ebertin says this combination is often associated with the deaths of relatives and I have found this to be true. In no way is that always the meaning but it will be seen at such times usually aspecting a difficult factor in the natal chart. It also occurs frequently with stillbirths.

(NE/PL)$_t$

Neptune/Pluto is a little like UR/NE only more weird. This combination is often associated with the supernatural and often deemed to be "out of this world." It involves a slow perception of something unaseen or unsuspected. It imparts, depending on what it aspects, a feeling of reverie or of sadness in a pining sort of way. Bliss or agony results depending solely on what it contacts.

(NE/MN)$_t$

This combination is best signified by a feeling of being in a group and finding yourself either under attack or totally snubbed. It's being disliked without knowing why. One hardly knows "why" when Neptune is involved, it doesn't work on the same logical principle as the rest of the planets. NE/MN is frequently also found in association with the sick, such as visits to the doctor.

(PL/MN)$_t$

Pluto/North Node represents association with large groups, not the close kind consisting of friends and family. It usually represents something shared in common with a large group of which you are a part.

We now present some example cases of these transiting midpoints aspecting the cosmogram. These are not inclusive and are intended to give the reader a feel for them. The CSI is especially helpful for more detailed and in-depth interpretations.

(UR/PL)$_t$	= SU/ME	a successful speech
	= JU	unexpected but coveted invitation to an event
	= M	day of big career promotion
(UR/NE)$_t$	= MO	unexpected and powerful spiritual experience
	= VE/MN	loved one wins an award
(UR/MN)$_t$	= MA	excitement with others - band concert
(NE/MN)$_t$	= A	hearing about a party - but not invited
	= M	doctor's visit
(NE/PL)$_t$	= VE/SA	agonizing romantic break-up
	= ME	hearing from someone from distant past
	= MN	sickness of relative
(PL/MN)$_t$	= A/M	political acceptance speech
	= UR	being at a gathering when a fight breaks out

About the Nodes

Many ephemerides give the true MN which shows stationary and retrograde movements. Others list the mean MN which moves at a steady pace, as if a clock's second hand were ticking around with no apparent changes in motion. Perhaps since the MN is symbolically an imaginary point rather than a moving body like a planet, the apparent motion is not necessary.

Margaret Millard, M.D.,[2] for one, found the mean node to be particularly important in genealogical chart work. The author finds the true node most valuable and uses it in the examples proffered herein. When ordering charts and computer printouts it is a good idea to check and see which type of nodal motion that company uses as a matter of course; you should request the one you prefer. It does make a difference in normal usage as they can be over a degree apart.

Endnotes:

1. Neil Michelson, *The American Midpoint Ephemeris 1991-1995* (San Diego: ACS Publications, 1985).

2. Margaret Millard M.D., *Casenotes of a Medical Astrologer* (York Beach, ME: Samuel Weiser, 1980),p.155.

5

Chiron Catalysts

"When I look up into the night skies and see the
work of your fingers — the moon and the stars
you have made..."

Psalms 8:3

I first became aware of the importance of Chiron while studying
transiting midpoints. This discovery led me on a six-year research
project which ultimately convinced me that Chiron was indeed a major
astrological entity. I do not claim to have discovered all the meanings
and ramifications of this new body but I do hope herein to add some
contribution to the already expanding knowledge compiled by others.

We have looked already briefly at the influence of Chiron transiting
alone and some of the results when Chiron contacts another point,
planet or midpoint. As we combine this body with the other outer
planets more pieces will be added to the Chiron puzzle. Several authors
have spoken of the blending effect of Chiron. There is some specula-
tion that this body does not possess rulership over any one particular
sign. Zane Stein[1] refers to the maverick nature of Chiron when conjunct a planet. I, too, see similar results using Chiron in combination
with the outer planets. "Catalyst" is a word that comes to mind over
and over in working with these combinations. Chiron seems to strengt-
hen and facilitate the work of Jupiter, Saturn, Uranus, Neptune and
Pluto, in addition to its own tentative place as a body of transition,
turning points and breakthroughs. In summary, it seems to show a
turning point involving the planet with which it combines. As we look
at examples of Chiron combined with each of these outer planets in a

45

transiting midpoint we will see how Chiron heightens the meaning of each.

Another aspect of Chiron relates to its computer-like ability to synthesize, by gathering a large number of divergent events and facts and bringing them together into a coherent whole. It's like finding the missing piece of a jigsaw puzzle and for the first time seeing the whole. Many experiences happen in life that make no sense while we are in their midst. We are mystified as to why they occurred. Then a major Chiron transiting midpoint like Pluto/Chiron, (PL/CH)$_t$, or Uranus/Chiron, (UR/CH)$_t$, comes along and suddenly the past takes on significance as we see its relation to the future. The why then becomes clear.

PL/CH A Powerful Combination

The most powerful transits are those involving the Pluto/Chiron midpoint. The keywords usually assigned to Pluto, such as "major," "intense," "fated" and "powerful," are rendered even more major, fated, intense and powerful with the addition of Chiron. It usually presages a major turning point or breakthrough in life. Hence, (PL/CH)$_t$ will often have the import of a direction. (PL/CH)$_t$ over a personal point, such as the Midheaven or Ascendant, or a midpoint containing one of these points is especially powerful.

We should also note that Chiron transits in particular seem to act like a bridge of some kind between the directions and the transits. I have not found this to be as true with the other outer planets. Chiron seems to link the transit to a direction involving a major planet in a person's chart. So that although the transits are essentially triggers of both the natal chart and the directions, Chiron seems more intricately related to the directed chart. Whatever Chiron contacts by transit seems directly related to the current direction even if it doesn't touch the exact same factor. Of course other writers have already suggested that Chiron is a bridge, especially as a bridge between the inner and outer planets. But Chiron may well be a bridge in more ways than one because it fits sensibly between the planets known since antiquity and those more recently discovered.

Transiting PL/CH emphasizes a change or turning point with an element of fate added - and from which there is no turning back. With

PL/CH the bridge behind you is burned or severed. It definitely shuts the door on one situation with a resounding bang. Looking at examples of PL/CH transits you begin to notice how Chiron brings to a head the event associated with the outer planet. Earlier in the book we used the PL/CH transit which started this pursuit. In that case it was (PL/-CH)$_t$ = A. This was by conjunction, the most potent of aspects. Three times in one month it touched a sensitive point in Mr. J.'s chart and Mr. J. experienced three intense and seemingly fated turning points involving his family members. Let's take a closer look at a few more cases of the transiting midpoint, (PL/CH)$_t$.

(PL/CH)$_t$ = ME/UR

In this instance an elderly lady had a dear pet cat which had been recently diagnosed as having cancer. The cat, in fact, had just had a biopsy to diagnose the extent of the spread of the disease and to explore avenues of possible treatment. The veterinarian did not offer much hope for its recovery. On the exact day of the (PL/CH)$_t$ aspect to the woman's ME/UR midpoint the doctor called saying that he had reviewed the laboratory report of the biopsy and that there had been a mistake in the original diagnosis. The cat had a rare benign disease that superficially resembled the more serious cancer. Her cat was going to be just fine. Here we have the ME/UR midpoint being aspected which could be interpreted as sudden or unexpected news. With Pluto it is major or strong. With the addition of Chiron it becomes a turning point or breakthrough. The door is now shut on the worry over the cancer. The reference to health is obvious, another attribute often assigned to Chiron. In fact, Chiron is often called a healer. Besides sudden news, the ME/UR midpoint can refer to a "renewal." I have seen Mercury midpoints involved before where pets are concerned. In another case we have the (PL/CH)$_t$ contacting the same natal ME/UR midpoint. On that day a young man received word of his acceptance into the college of his choice. Again sudden news brought with it a turning point in life.

Several examples of transiting PL/CH hitting natal factors are shown below. In a few of these examples other directions and transits may have been operating, but often the PL/CH midpoint was the only evident activity in effect on a particular day. Even if other factors are

47

operating, $(PL/CH)_t$ [and $(UR/CH)_t$] are often found present at major turning points in life. Although $(PL/CH)_t$ is usually positive, there are times when it can be devastating and this seems especially so when it is teamed with a midpoint involving the Moon. However even though contacting a problematical midpoint the transiting PL/CH is not always perceived as difficult. For example, under a transit of PL/CH to VE/SA, suffering in love would be an expected experience. But in one case a man heard from a love from his past. He found that she had moved closer and would be able to resume a friendship based on more than occasional letter writing. Here $(PL/CH)_t$ shows as a major turning point, with VE/SA a love from the past. Pluto alone dredges up the past and this particular combination occurs often in the resumption of a past relationship.

$(PL/CH)_t = M/JU$

On the day of this aspect a government worker received an outstanding job rating and a promotion with pay. Here we have Jupiter standing for good fortune, with the Midheaven, representing one's career and success, contacted by the $(PL/CH)_t$, a major turning point.

$(PL/CH)_t = M/SA$

The M/SA midpoint often points to career difficulty. In one case a woman lost a chance for a promotion, a real career setback for her.

Before looking at the rest of the $(PL/CH)_t$ examples it is noted that all of these transiting midpoints, including the Jupiters and Saturns under discussion have contacted the midpoint exactly. There was no orb to be considered. For example, if the ME/UR midpoint is, say, 13 Virgo 45, then when it is mentioned that a transiting midpoint contacts it, that contact is exact, i.e., 13° 45' with variations of a second or two at most. This exactness of transiting midpoints is phenomenal to say the least and will prove to be of the utmost importance in the discussion of chart rectification in Chapter 6.

Examples of $(PL/CH)_t$ on the day of an event:

$(PL/CH)_t$ = MN/M   hearing about an unexpected inheritance
$(PL/CH)_t$ = MN/M   first date with future spouse

48

$(PL/CH)_t$	= CH/A	birth of a daughter
$(PL/CH)_t$	= NE/A	birth in the family
$(PL/CH)_t$	= MA/PL	a major career success
$(PL/CH)_t$	= SU/UR	an engagement
$(PL/CH)_t$	= VE/PL	another engagement
$(PL/CH)_t$	= SU/VE	birth of a son
$(PL/CH)_t$	= MN	an engagement
$(PL/CH)_t$	= JU	winning a championship game
$(PL/CH)_t$	= SU/MA	injury to a male relative
$(PL/CH)_t$	= MO/PL	a man's child breaks his arm
$(PL/CH)_t$	= MO/A	death of one's father-in-law
$(PL/CH)_t$	= MO/A	injury to a younger brother
$(PL/CH)_t$	= CH/A	purchase of first car
$(PL/CH)_t$	= SU	winning an award
$(PL/CH)_t$	= MO/MN	a sister's marriage
$(PL/CH)_t$	= JU/PL	a brother's marriage

NE/CH Agony without the Ecstasy

If Neptune represents bliss or agony, then Chiron makes it doubly so, and although Neptune can mean feelings sublime, the downside is usually more evident. At least in most lives ecstasy is rare, feelings of pain, defeat, and disillusionment being sadly much more prevalent. If $(PL/CH)_t$ represents the most powerful of the transiting midpoints then surely $(NE/CH)_t$ is the most agonizing. A look at the keywords gives a clue as to what to expect from this transit: Chiron, a turning point or transition that is somehow weird, slow, agonizing or painful, and to be sure one for which there is no explanation. NE/CH isn't just misery, it's miserable misery, probably made more so by the Chiron catalyst of a permanently closing door. The door that is yet to be opened is too illusive to be seen at the time of the transit. All you generally see is the pain, suffering or heartbreak. NE/CH is often seen as "dissolving." Rather than closing a door, $(NE/CH)_t$ seems to dissolve the door in a peculiar, painful or mysterious way.

$(NE/CH)_t = VE/NE$

The following example is of an event by semisquare — not too potent — signifying a disappointment in love — a typical VE/NE meaning. It was also a strange love experience, another VE/NE meaning. A woman heard from a man she hadn't seen in quite awhile, but for whom she had quite positive feelings. He called and they had a nice talk and plans were made for the following evening. The next day he called, acted "cool" and cancelled the date for "no earthly reason." This is a typically Neptunian situation and the incident certainly dissolved her former good feeling toward him.

(NE/CH)$_t$ is frequently found at times of injuries and even deaths. Injuries involving burns are common. It is also a factor in strange experiences like robberies, arrests and other brushes with the law and criminal elements. Everyone is familiar with that old Neptune feeling when the blinking red light atop a police vehicle is following you! In injuries, disease and other kinds of similar situations, there is usually something "peculiar" connected with it. The following illustrate the effects of transiting NE/CH.

(NE/CH)$_t$ = M/A	the day of a final divorce
(NE/CH)$_t$ = MO	death of father
(NE/CH)$_t$ = VE	one's child injured in a fire
(NE/CH)$_t$ = VE/JU	injury to a child, also a burn
(NE/CH)$_t$ = ME/NE	a daughter breaks herarm
(NE/CH)$_t$ = UR/PL	a brother is arrested
(NE/CH)$_t$ = NE/CH	arrest
(NE/CH)$_t$ = MO/SA	a son is injured
(NE/CH)$_t$ = A/JU	the day a house is robbed
(NE/CH)$_t$ = A/SA	injured in a freak accident
(NE/CH)$_t$ = VE/PL	death of mother

Though there must be some occasional "good" aspect involving the transiting NE/CH midpoint, I have not yet observed one.

SA/CH Sometimes Life is Hard

If (NE/CH)$_t$ dissolves, then (SA/CH)$_t$ shatters. Saturn is "just the cold, hard facts ma'am." The door is shut, with a bang; and you know it — no mystery here. Saturn with Chiron is a sobering influence, a combination that brings one down to earth. No vague wondering about the door even if it's there as with (NE/CH)$_t$. This effect is definite; you can see the door right there in front of you and it's closed. You have to face it. Still sometimes we need our feet on the ground and the transiting SA/CH midpoint does this very well. Saturn/Chiron often closes a door that needs to be closed. Sometimes it says that the past is over and you need to take another direction. More than anything else, however, SA/CH is physical. Often it's a physical injury or illness. Frequently it involves the teeth and bones — old friends of Saturn. At other times, if you are on a wrong path, or "flying high," a SA/CH transit comes along and says stop, hold everything right there. It's sometimes like a little illness, a little injury, or a little pain that is enough to slow us down and bring us to our senses. It's a smack on the bottom of a two-year-old, very physical and very effective. Still these are daily events, not earthquakes, and they help us keep things in perspective - another of Saturn's tasks. With Chiron is added the element of a transition or turning point. Especially do we find the stern teacher or taskmaster when Saturn and Chiron are combined. In its effect the (SA/CH)$_t$ midpoint is on a par with the other Saturn midpoints.

Some examples:

(SA/CH)$_t$	= A/ME	a sister was ill
(SA/CH)$_t$	= MA/SA	a dental patient has a root canal performed
(SA/CH)$_t$	= SU/NE	injury from a mild burn
(SA/CH)$_t$	= SU/SA	a day on which a male relative died
(SA/CH)$_t$	= MO/PL	the end of a relationship
(SA/CH)$_t$	= UR/PL	a son falls off his bicycle and is injured
(SA/CH)$_t$	= SA/NE	being in a dangerous situation
(SA/CH)$_t$	= VE/SA	a generally miserable social evening
(SA/CH)$_t$	= SA/PL	a broken hand
(SA/CH)$_t$	= SA	fight with a friend
(SA/CH)$_t$	= MA	a brother chips a tooth

UR/CH Oh, Boy!

This expression is what comes to mind when studying the transiting Uranus/Chiron midpoint. This midpoint invokes an image of hands clapping together joyfully. Although Uranus alone can bring difficult events as well as joy, depending on the combination of factors it aspects, there appear to be little or no negative events under this transiting combination. It is a joy to see a good UR/CH aspect coming up in a chart; it lifts the one's spirits after having dealt with the more challenging NE/CH and SA/CH heavies. Like UR/PL it also signals a joy but it's even happier. There is more of a thrill associated with UR/CH. Watch it transit your chart to see the truth of this statement. It's joy and success even without Jupiter. It's like hearing that you just won a lottery — Oh, Boy! Now for a look at some events on the day of a transit of UR/CH in a typical cosmogram:

$(UR/CH)_t$ = MA/SA   making a team
$(UR/CH)_t$ = A/MA   sister's marriage
$(UR/CH)_t$ = JU/NE   marriage
$(UR/CH)_t$ = JU/UR   birth of a cousin
$(UR/CH)_t$ = VE/SA   sister's engagement
$(UR/CH)_t$ = M/JU   job promotion
$(UR/CH)_t$ = SU/MA   accepted at Officer Training School
$(UR/CH)_t$ = M   meeting the future spouse at a party
$(UR/CH)_t$ = A/UR   family member wins a political election
$(UR/CH)_t$ = VE/UR   a wife receives inheritance
$(UR/CH)_t$ = MO   unexpected receipt of a beautiful gift
$(UR/CH)_t$ = VE/CH   a daughter's engagement
$(UR/CH)_t$ = A/JU   a sister's engagement
$(UR/CH)_t$ = SU/CH   a father receives favorable notoriety
$(UR/CH)_t$ = ME/NE   winning the lead in a play

JU/CH The Best of the Jupiters

This midpoint is slightly more potent in effect than the other Jupiter combinations. Perhaps that's because even though less potent we tend to remember and magnify in our minds happy events that are also turning points even if they are not real overpowering in their effect. Besides denoting happiness, Jupiter transiting with Chiron brings good fortune. It's best described as just the right thing happening at just the right time. And it is not just to personal points and planets that we particularly notice $(JU/CH)_t$. Witness $(JU/CH)_t$ = UR. Just when one job had ended and a lady was wondering what to do next, she got word of a new job possibility that was perfect for her. A door opened for her which was fortunate. Incidentally, this transit activated a direction to Uranus indicating that it was more than a daily event. It triggered a happy career opening. Other examples of (JU/CH)$_t$ events on the day of the exact aspect are:

(JU/CH)$_t$ = JU	a birth in the family
(JU/CH)$_t$ = MO	an engagement
(JU/CH)$_t$ = SA	a marriage
(JU/CH)$_t$ = A/MA	a good business deal
(JU/CH)$_t$ = VE	sister receives an award
(JU/CH)$_t$ = SU/UR	job promotion
(JU/CH)$_t$ = M/PL	a happy meeting
(JU/CH)$_t$ = ME	good news via a telephone call
(JU/CH)$_t$ = NE/PL	getting an 'A' on a test
(JU/CH)$_t$ = PL	opportunity for leadership

CH/MN Turning Tides

This combination is less understood than the foregoing as it is more elusive and more difficult to describe. The combination by itself indicates a door opening or closing to a group or association of which you are a part. Or perhaps it signifies an opening to a new group of people. The MN definitely has something to do with associations that play a part in the working out of your individual destiny. In the chart of a politician the transiting CH/MN = M/PL indicated that the tide (his constituents) had turned against him. He attended a rally and was booed by former supporters. Another gentlemen, with (CH/MN)$_t$ stationary on his MA/JU midpoint became popular overnight after a successful speech at a club meeting.

The MN doesn't always just symbolize groups of people but it very definitely is associated with what some writers would call "karmic ties." Hence, an element of fate is associated with the MN. In comparing charts of two or more persons, the MN readily signifies definite common ties. For example, your natal MO/MN may be on your wife's or mother's Sun or Moon. Your SU/MN may be on an important personal part in a male relative's chart or your VE/MN in the same relation in a female relative's chart. This discussed in more detail in the chapter on synastry.

Both the MN and Chiron are associated with relationships and I would suspect that by transit this combination is shown less on a personal level and more in relation to your important contacts with groups of people. It has been discussed here how Chiron acts in transiting midpoints. In the next chapter it will be shown how their incredible accuracy can be used to rectify charts.

Endnotes:

1. Zane Stein, "The Meaning of Chiron." Lecture: Astrologer's Guild of America (NY, Dec. 1979).

6

A Bridge to Rectification

"The heavens are telling the glory of God; they are a marvelous
display of his craftsmanship. Day and night they keep on telling
about God. Without a sound or word, silent in the skies, their mes-
sage reaches out to all the world."

Psalms 19:1-4

Rectification is admittedly one of the most difficult tasks in cosmobiology. In fact it is so difficult that few attempt it and succeed with
more than a very general degree of accuracy. Yet with the power and
exactness of transiting midpoints, especially some of the Chiron midpoints, it is possible to rectify many charts to the minute or less and
later verification has proven them correct. This can be a tedious task
but the results are rewarding and worth the effort. With transiting
midpoints one can pinpoint the actual birth time with amazing accuracy. It is best to start with three midpoint printout charts for the day of
birth. If the time is completely unknown, use 6AM, noon, and 6PM for
a broad overall view of the day. If an approximate time is known, use
two sets of midpoints for times on either side of the range of estimated
time. The job is considerably easier for estimates such as "sometime in
the morning" or "late at night." For a "late evening" birth, one might
use two midpoint printouts for, say, 8PM and midnight. If someone
says, "I was born around 11AM," then use 10:30AM and noon, leaving
enough leeway on either side. It might also be helpful to have a printout for exactly 11AM.

55

With these natal midpoint printouts once obtained, take a one- to two-year period of time and have the person select 10 to 15 events during that time period for which the exact dates are known. Another method is to choose 10 to 15 dates in the persons life which correlate with significant events in their lives. For this accuracy is needed, so "sometime in May" would not be good enough.

Specification Sheets

At the top of any type of paper, write two or three of the dates and the event that occurred briefly on each day. It helps to have the exact date listed if you need to refer to ephemerides for additional information or to check your accuracy in recording the information. Under each event list a column of appropriate outer planets and transiting midpoints depending on the nature of the event. For a happy occasion, say an engagement, list PL, NE, CH, UR, JU, UR/PL, UR/CH, PL/CH and, of course, most of the Jupiter midpoints. Also include NE/PL and UR/NE as these can be found in both positive and negative situations. In addition, for a happy event you might add MA/JU. Even though Mars midpoints aren't as accurate in this particular approach as the others, they are often found in certain situations and could prove helpful to the task at hand.

Example Specification Sheet
June 20th   Marriage Proposal

PL
UR
CH
JU
NE

UR/PL
UR/CH
PL/CH
UR/NE
NE/PL

JU/CH
JU/NE
JU/PL
JU/UR

MA/JU

One could list several of these midpoints and planets on one sheet of paper but it is best not to use the back of the sheets as it makes comparison much more difficult if you have to keep turning the pages over to check information. Now beside each entry write in the sign and degree of that planet or midpoint on the day in question. It is helpful to list all the entries the way they are found listed in a 45-degree ephemeris. This way none of the semisquares and sesquiquadrates, which are just as important, are missed. So if Pluto on the day in question is listed at 17 Scorpio 10, it is written the way it is shown in a 45° sequence or sort (17 Scorpio 10 = 47° 10' - 45° = 2° 10'C where C stands for Cardinal), which is as 2° 10'C. If the transiting midpoint of UR/PL is at 10 Pisces 30, it is written as 25° 30'C. When using 45° notation you don't need to include a letter such as C for cardinal or F for fixed, but one can do so to avoid confusion. Now let us consider a difficult event such as a death in a family for which the choice of planets and points to list would be a little different. Here one should include the transiting Saturn midpoints, and of course (NE/CH)$_t$. You might want to include in this type of event the midpoint (MA/SA)$_t$. For an accident or operation include (MA/UR)$_t$.

Example Specification Sheet
April 20th Father's death
PL
UR
CH
NE
SA

PL/CH
NE/CH
UR/NE
NE/PL

SA/CH
SA/PL
SA/UR
SA/NE

MA/SA

With practice, a feel can be developed as to which elements to include depending on the nature of the event. Sometimes, surprisingly, it is well to list Neptune for happy occasions, especially if they are of the blissful type. Always list PL/CH for every event because it is so powerful. The following Specification sheet is for a Miss T. and includes three meaningful events in her life occurring within one year. In actual practice more than three events should be considered.

Spec Sheet for Miss T.

3/1 Marriage Proposal	6/18 Job Success	9/12 Death of a Pet
PL 5°01'C	PL	PL
NE	NE	NE 14°50'C
UR 28°18'C	UR 27°30'C	UR
JU 14°48'C	JU	SA
CH	CH	CH
PL/CH 4°15'F	PL/CH	PL/CH 6°01'C
UR/CH 6°05'C	UR/CH 14°53'C	NE/CH 28°28C
UR/PL	UR/PL	
		UR/NE 14°10'C

UR/NE	UR/NE	NE/PL
NE/PL	NE/PL	
		SA/PL
JU/CH 28°30'C	JU/CH	SA/NE
JU/UR	JU/UR 5°05'C	SA/CH
JU/PL	JU/PL	SA/UR 4°11'F
MA/JU 6°10'C	MA/JU 28°35'C	MA/SA 14°50'C

The list contains only those planets and midpoints relevant to the discussion at hand so that it easier to locate them. Once you have filled in all the specification sheets go through and lightly circle those that are very close in degree and list those that are alike on another sheet called a common. Under each degree that you find repeated list the date and the planet or midpoint that accompanies it. In Miss T.'s list, JU/CH under marriage proposal at 28°30'C is taken together with NE/CH under death of pet at 28°28'C. But note that Uranus at 28°18' under marriage proposal is not included in this group because it is 10' from the other two. To take advantage of the accuracy of this method list together only those factors with a difference of less than 5' between them. Do this for each group that you find alike. From Miss T.'s chart we show below what you might have listed on the common.

@ 14° 53'	@ 28° 30'	@ 4° 10'F or 34° 10'
9/12 MA/SA 14° 50'	3/1 JU/CH 28° 30'	9/12 SA/UR 4°11'
6/18 UR/CH 14° 53'	9/12 PL/CH 28° 28'	3/1 PL/CH 4° 15'
3/1 JU 14° 48'	6/18 MA/JU 28° 35'	
9/12 NE 14° 50'		

Once you have done this necessary preparation you are really ready for research. What you will be particularly looking for are degrees that could signify the Moon, Ascendant and Midheaven or midpoint combinations with one of these personal points.

It is easier to start by looking for the Moon and Moon midpoints first. The closer the estimate of the birth time, the easier it will be since it considerably narrows down the number of degrees in which the Moon can be found.

One of the first things to do with the common sheet is to eliminate those points and midpoints that are already known from the person's basic chart. For example on the common consider the listing at 34° 10' or 4° 10'F. If these group around, say, the JU/PL midpoint then you can eliminate JU/PL from your sheet since you already know what it stands for.

34'10°
9/12 SA/UR 4° 11'
3/1   PL/CH 4° 15'

You may find a point listed such as the Sun or Venus and you can likewise cross them off as well. What is left then is several pages of very important points in the person's chart. Some of them is most probably the Moon, Ascendant and Midheaven and some are combinations of these with midpoints. The closer a knowledge of the actual birthtime the easier it will be to spot these. If you only need to rectify within a matter of a few minutes than you may need not to go any further. If you discover a point which at this time may be the Moon, try combining it with midpoints and see how it works. If you then come up with other midpoints that are also listed in the common also turn up, you are probably on to something.

Another approach is to study the person's chart for the day of birth and see if any planets that are just a few degrees apart. Suppose for example a person has JU at 0° Sagittarius and UR at 2° Sagittarius. It doesn't matter whether the planets that are a few degree apart are in different signs just so long as they are in the same quadruplicity.) So if Jupiter is at 0° Sagittarius, Uranus could be at 2° Sagittarius, Virgo, Pisces or Gemini. Since these are about two degrees apart their midpoints would be about 1° apart. Now suppose that in the common you come up with several repeating points about a degree apart, as follows.

<u>@ 5° 0'</u>   <u>@ 6° 0'</u>
3/1 PL 5° 10'   and   3/1 JU 6° 05'
6/18 JU/UR 5° 05'   9/12 PL 6° 01'
                          3/1 MA/JU 6° 10'

In this case one should find a degree which when combined with both JU and UR in the natal chart will give 5° and 6° respectively.

JU/? = 5° or (20° F)
UR/? = 6° or (21° F)

In this case, 10° of a fixed sign (40° in the 45° sequence), when added to both Jupiter and Uranus to form midpoints will give the required answer. So 10° F is probably the Moon, Ascendant or Midheaven. If it is close to what the Moon could be you are probably right on target. If you already have an approximate Moon at some other location then this is probably the Ascendant or Midheaven.

Next see whether 10° F is shown in other combinations in the common sheet. For example, you might find that trying 10° F with the native's Pluto at 15° Libra gives a midpoint at 27° 30'. Notice that this is the Uranus degree on June 18 of the example.

If you determine that 10° of a fixed sign is either the Midheaven or Ascendant, then there are about 8 total possibilities for 10 degrees of any fixed sign being the Ascendant or Midheaven on any one day. Using a precise table of houses for the location of birth you can locate these eight possibilities and also list the times. Below is listed the sidereal times on the date in question and the eight possibilities of the Ascendant or Midheaven being 10° of a fixed sign at Washington, D.C.

<u>ST</u>
1:50 M = 29° Aries   A = <u>10° Leo</u>
2:31 M = <u>10° Taurus</u> A = 18° Leo
8:50 M = <u>10° Leo</u>   A = 4° Scorpio
9:20 M = 17° Leo   A = <u>10° Scorpio</u>
14:31 M = <u>10° Scorpio</u>   A = 17° Capricorn
15:50 M = 29° Scorpio   A = <u>10° Aquarius</u>

61

19:41 M = 23° Cap   A = 10° Taurus
20:50 M = 10° Aquarius   A = 12° Gemini

Having gone thus far, your ability to zero in on two or three possible birth times depends on the closeness of the original guesses. One of the Midheaven or Ascendant degrees at 10 degrees fixed may also stand out in the common. In this case at 15:50 ST the Midheaven is at 29° Scorpio and the Ascendant is at 10° F. You may find 29 degrees of a fixed sign (or 14° C) listed in the specifications or common sheet. UR/NE is at that degree on September 12.

This may seem complicated at first and these examples are given to show what to look for and what can be found. No two rectifications will go in the same way. Sometimes you will take blind alleys and other times things will "pop out" rather easily. I have yet to find one instance where at least one of the selected midpoints doesn't have a direct relation to the chart being rectified. It's just a matter of "playing" with the specification sheets and trying various combinations. In this regard some charts are much easier to work with than others. One chart literally took months of playing with. The combinations never came out quite right. Only the day of birth was certain with no inkling of the hour. As it turned out the native's Moon was almost conjunct another planet thus making it very tricky. On the other hand I have rectified other charts in a matter of hours.

The hardest situation is when you only have the date and no time. Sometimes in such cases known major midpoints in a native's chart, such as JU/PL or JU/UR, in the natives chart that only vary a few degrees a day can help narrow the time to AM or PM. Suppose a person's JU/UR midpoint is between 15° 51' and 15 Sagittarius 57. If 15 Sagittarius 52 (0° 52'F or 30° 52') repeat often in the specifications or in the common then this probably equates with the JU/UR midpoint and so the birth would have occurred in the morning. If instead 15° 57' comes ups repeatedly, then a late PM birth is indicated.

As you work with the specifications and common sheets you will find many clues like this one. Here just knowing if the birth occurred in the AM or PM would help to narrow down the position of the Moon considerably. Once you've located the position of the Moon, you are halfway there as then the Ascendant and Midheaven can be narrowed down to within a half an hour of the birth time. If you believe you have fixed the Moon, try combining it with the other planets to form natal midpoints. If several of these midpoints are already found in the specifications and fit the occasion then you probably have it!

Moon at _____
<u>Moon Midpoints</u>
SU/MO
MO/ME
MO/VE
MO/MA
MO/JU
MO/SA
MO/UR
MO/NE
MO/PL
MO/CH
MO/MN

It is vitally important to be aware of the major midpoint meanings and what results to expect with them to avoid confusion. For example, the PL/M midpoint in a person's chart represents success or achievement. Although there might Moon or Venus which involves the usual "love" indications, this midpoint is found repeatedly in love encounters. Another point to keep in mind is that although a repeating specification is usually significant in a person's chart, it is not always so. A particular axis in the chart may contain points or midpoints which are significant in other ways in a person's life. This is particularly true if the events listed would have affected another person. However repeating specifications are significant in a person's chart and they may represent a "shared" midpoint between two people. I have often found a repeating point in a specification sheet which does not seem to fit only to discover that is was an important point in the spouse's chart. So it's good to keep these little discrepancies in mind when working with the specifications. In fact it would be rare to have more than two or three active aspects listed in any column for a particular date no matter how "big" the event. The major CH midpoints, PL/CH, UR/-CH, NE/CH, SA/CH and JU/CH along with UR/PL and sometimes NE/PL or UR/NE are the most potent significators of events in the specifications and the most useful midpoints to incorporate in the lists. They are inevitably involved in "big time" happenings since such events usually signify some sort of turning point in life. Not only are Chiron and the Chiron midpoints important and helpful for rectification but they can be used in like manner in studying daily transits. Take any important day, such as an important meeting, wedding, party, etc., and list all the main transits on that day including the transiting midpoints PL, NE, UR, SA, CH, JU, UR/PL, UR/NE, PL/CH, UR/CH, JU/UR, JU/PL, JU/CH, (NE/CH, SA/CH, and the Saturns for a "difficult" day) and I guarantee that at least two and sometimes more of these will touch an important point or midpoint in a person's chart. These contacts will be exact! Even daily events of significance will be shown. These are the representatives of events. And they work.

7

Transitions and Turning Points

"He assigned the moon to mark the months, and the sun to mark the days."

Psalms 104 : 19

Part I: Chiron and the Inner Planets

With the inner planets we can also speak of direct Chiron transits having an effect. When Chiron contacts an outer planet in the natal chart not too much action is seen unless a direction is being activated or there are other correlating transits. The action with the outer planets is observed mainly in their combinations as transiting midpoints and when they contact a personal point, planet or midpoint in the chart. Although not always as exact as the transiting midpoints or transits to midpoints, these transits of Chiron do in fact herald transitions, breakthroughs and turning points in life. They are not always exact for the day of a main event, but these events are never one day occurrences anyway. Instead they tend to evolve over a period of time such as when someone moves, makes new contacts, takes a new job or undergoes relationship changes. However when Chiron contacts one of the personal planets, points or midpoints, a daily transiting event related to the larger event will usually occur. In fact since directions often herald many larger changes in life, Chiron can be found as a key or trigger that marks the point whereby the new situation becomes a permanent change rather than a tentative one. For example, you make a new acquaintance and whether or not that person develops into a permanent friend or becomes a person who will strongly affect your life will depend on many factors. A triggering transit where this turning point from acquaintance to friendship solidifies is often found with Chiron. Several different combinations can refer to similar types of events and some events that are alike can be expressed in many different ways. It is therefore difficult to predict that such and such will occur on such and such an event day. The most a cosmobiologist can do is read and interpret the map (the cosmogram) and the road signs (transits and directions) on the path of life, pointing out obstacles and difficulties as well as opportunities for success and happiness. In this next chapter a summary of what Chiron presages when it touches one of these personal planets or points in the chart is presented. In addition Chiron is combined with each of the personal planets and points and the meanings of these newly created midpoints are discussed. This is by no means inclusive. More data is obviously needed. The reader may accept or reject these ideas as new research warrants. With that thought in mind let us take a more personal look.

Chiron and the Sun

According to most texts the Sun represents the life, the body, vitality and in many cases the male principle in general. In the chart of a male the Sun often represents the physical, whereas in that of a woman it often represents a male in her life and, surprisingly, often represents the most important thing in her life, whether it be career, children or even a man. For both sexes the Sun in midpoint combinations is related to relationships with other males. Sometimes with males or females various planets or combinations touching the Sun will signify some personal success — a visible outer success in the world as opposed to the Midheaven which may indicate more one's soul feelings or soul growth in relation to success. Very frequently Chiron aspecting the Sun by one of the hard aspects is the main trigger of a larger event. Hence Chiron to the Sun will often seem more important than Chiron to the other planets and points. Especially important is the transit of an outer planet or transiting midpoint transiting the same degree or midpoint axis as the Sun on that day. When Chiron is in the same degree as the Sun, and in hard aspect, this then becomes a major transit or direction.

Chiron touching the Sun by transit often indicates a new contact with a male in a woman's chart. Likewise in a male's chart Chiron aspecting the Sun also seems to indicate a new woman or at most a new "love." This result is surprising as one might think that in a man's chart, at least a new love would be shown by a contact to the Moon or Venus. But in both charts, male's or female's, a contact to Venus often signifies something happening to a loved one and Chiron to the Moon often has much more to do with feelings. Chiron transiting the Sun is also found in any major life event, good or bad, which points out that the ancients truly knew the importance of the Sun as the timer and source of vitality in one's chart. The Sun also represents the body and any aspect of Chiron by transit or direction will often signal a health crisis. It not just an individual crisis either. When Chiron touches the Sun the health crisis often relates to a member of the immediate family. The Sun/Chiron midpoint, SU/CH, aspected by transits of outer planets or transiting midpoints or directions seems to have the nature of SU/UR more than any other combination. It usually signifies something unexpected and sudden. Here the Sun takes on its usual role of representing the male principle. In a male chart it often refers to himself or a male friend or relative. And likewise in a female chart it often signifies the same. Incidentally we often find that these midpoints involving the personal planets or points represent a person in your life. This is especially so in genealogical work. So that combinations with the Moon and Venus often represent women and with the Sun and Mars represent males.

In this regard the Sun represents the native, and in combination with Chiron or any other planet often represents another person important to the native as shown in the natal chart. In the transiting chart it represents someone who is important to the native or who is significant in the native's life at that time. At one time SU/CH might represent the father, another a brother, or a male boss. For example, consider $(JU/PL)_t$ = SU/CH in a woman's chart. On that day her husband received a promotion at work. Incidentally the husband's chart on that day was under the effect of $(UR/CH)_t$ = SU. It was a good turning point for him, too.

Chiron and the Moon

Chiron and the Moon is tricky. There is often something sad about its effects because they touch the emotions in some way. This same

67

response shows up occasionally with contacts of Pluto and the Moon. There is usually a more hidden response when Chiron contacts the Moon than the more open event seen with contacts to the Sun. Perhaps because the Moon relates to the inner life it is not as easy to interpret these contacts. Although the Moon is traditionally associated with the mother, in this case it often refers to children as well, as does Mercury. For example, Chiron conjuncted a man's Moon on the day he started work as a counselor with young children, signifying a turning point in his feelings or perhaps a breakthrough of some kind in relation to children. In her book, *Secrets From a Stargazer's Notebook*,[1] Debbi Kempton-Smith writes that her mother died when Chiron passed over her Moon. Here we have the sadness and also the traditional meaning of the Moon as mother. Another person entered a hospital with Chiron opposite the Moon. Again a certain sadness was experienced along with a regression to an earlier level of dependency. In a similar case a woman experienced much sorrow and grief over a child when Chiron was contacting her Moon — more sadness and children shown again.

The combined midpoint of the Moon and Chiron, MO/CH, may have the flavor of MO/VE with a slight twist. Moon/Venus recall signifies great feelings of love, devotion and tenderness. MO/CH does likewise with a little more excitement than just a rather bland "devotion." This is an exciting combination relating to feelings. More than MO/VE what seems to be in action is a combination of both MO/VE and MO/UR.

Any direction involving the Moon and Chiron is particularly important and often involves a major new love coming into one's life, true to the symbology of a "turning point" in feelings. Especially is this evident in MO_s = CH and MO_s to the midpoint UR/CH. Very often a future mate appears under one of these directions.

Moon/Chiron contacts by transit or direction are very personal, and when found in midpoints they can indicate either a female or especially a child or children. MO/CH often indicates a sibling, particularly a younger sibling.

Chiron and Mercury

Mercury is associated with speech, news and communication. It also strongly correlates in midpoints with young people in general and brothers and sisters in particular. This coincides with Gemini the traditional sign ruled by Mercury, Gemini and with its traditional house, the third, ruler of siblings. If the Moon can stand for children then Mercury would have a special affinity for teenagers. In combinations with other planets Mercury also denotes brothers and sisters-in-law as well as cousins. So when observing a contact to ME/CH it is difficult to predict whether there might be news of some kind or whether a sibling is indicated. It work both ways. ME/CH, however, more than any of the other Mercury combinations in midpoints, more commonly refers to the latter — one's kin. Chiron touching Mercury by transit and direction usually triggers news that brings changes with it, while Chiron, or any other outer planet touching ME/CH, is involves family members. Once again Chiron is seen to lean toward "relationships" in meaning. There are occasions when the transit of Chiron over natal Mercury indicates turning points which do not necessarily result from "news." For example, CH =ME frequently shows during moves, particularly those that affect a younger person in the family.

PL_t = ME/CH in one case of a mother affected her children. In another, PL_t = ME/CH brought about a surprising telephone call to a young man. In another situation a woman experienced CH_t = ME on the day her sister and family moved to a new home.

Remembering that a Chiron transit is just that — a transit, its significance and importance will be determined by the directions it triggers. A transit of JU = $(ME/SA)_r$ can be interpreted as saying good-bye or as fortunate separation. In transit by itself this could mean the ending of a vacation or the saying good-bye to someone going on a short trip. However in one situation this occurred under a direction. A woman was involved in a miserable situation with a man and she extricated herself on the very day that transiting Chiron contacted her Mercury which triggered the direction JU_s = ME/SA in effect at that time.

Chiron and Venus

It may come as a surprise that Chiron to Venus often indicates a change of environment, such as a vacation or a visit to a place considered more beautiful than one's normal scenery. Venus when aspected by a transit of Chiron shows up as relating to loved ones in general rather than just to females. Often a Chiron to Venus aspect will be due on the day of a party or a happy gathering of friends. Sometimes it includes a hidden Mercury-type element involving communication, such as a pleasant conversation with others or good news from or about loved ones. Sometimes this aspect is also found at times of moves and births.

The VE/CH midpoint has an element of VE/UR, a stepping up or excitement in love yet with a more serious intent. One's feelings with VE/CH seem more genuine as opposed to the more physical side of VE/UR or the obsessive quality of VE/PL. As with other Chiron combinations, VE/CH often represents a person, especially a loved one in one's life.

Chiron and Mars

Over and over I have seen transits of Chiron to Mars representing a new job. Above other meanings this one stands out whether the native is male or female, young or old. It makes you wonder if Mars doesn't play a larger part in career or occupation than previously thought. Michel Gauquelin[2] found Mars to be prevalent in certain occupations. He observed that Mars was significant in certain sectors of the natal charts of soldiers, soldiering being naturally a Martian occupation. But Mars mean more than a career as a soldier. It also represents energy which is often directed into a new area (Chiron), and hence a transition. Mars in midpoint with Chiron is a little different and more related to the traditional meanings of the planet. It is very much concerned with the male principle and any outer planet contacting MA/CH often pertains to a male in your life. It can also refer to injuries associated with Mars like cuts, and wounds, with fire and so forth. For a female there is often an element of excitement when a planet is touched by a MA/CH transit in her chart. While Chiron was contacting MA/CH in a woman's chart her brother was involved in a serious accident. More significantly it represented a turning point for him as well. Transiting Uranus to the MA/CH midpoint in a woman's chart can represent a different kind of excitement — a first date with a man! As you work with Chiron and the inner planets you develop a feel for what to expect. A Chiron transit is not to be overrated just because it is a newly discovered body. Neither should it be underrated. It is a transit — no more no less, and in transit operates just like Pluto, Neptune, Saturn, Uranus and sometimes Jupiter. It combines with the other planets and sensitive points in the same way. What is not yet available with Chiron is the years of experience needed to properly interpret it. Further work with this little body will help in understanding it better. Now let us turn our attention to Chiron in combination with the personal points in the hope of augmenting our overall knowledge.

Part II: Chiron and the Personal Points

The Ascendant, Midheaven and M/A midpoint are so important they really deserve a separate section. In the cosmogram they represent the soul or heart of a person's being. They are the most personal of contacts and from a cosmobiologists point of view their meanings loom larger than previously believed. As far as transits go they are most important when combined with Chiron contacts as they show the most potent effects. When activated in directions they are very powerful and especially so when associated with Chiron. A definite visible event occurs when they are contacted by Chiron and also at the same time a subtle unseen change in one's feelings or perceptions manifests, some little growth in consciousness. Chiron opens a door to a new way of looking at our lives and our innermost selves.

The Ascendant

The Ascendant has always been associated with one's environment by cosmobiologists. Also called the rising sign represents a window through which you see the world and the world sees you. In conjunction with other sensitive points and planets it represents the personality. However, this is such a personal point it doesn't just represent all 'them' out there — the people in your environment - but in particular it represents you in relation to "them." The Ascendant also has a lot to do with one's health. It represents the physical body as opposed to the

Midheaven which inclines more to the mind or ego. In other words the Ascendant is one's physical being in the physical environment. Because of this, contacts to it are more obvious in the form of outward events than are contacts to the Midheaven.

It happens often that the description of the personality through the Ascendant is indicated by the next sign. For example, in your chart, you may have Scorpio rising but you tend to look and act more like a textbook Sagittarian.

There are two and possibly more explanations for this. It could well be that since the physical body and environment are such a large part of life that the Ascendant should be broadened to include the next sign. Yet in practice the exact degree of the Ascendant is important and does not lose its significance and power throughout the native's life. It is not the degree which often doesn't fit the individual description of the sign. This anomaly could not be caused by adhering to the tropical instead of the sidereal zodiac since with the sidereal one would more likely go back one sign rather than forward. And in such cases as these, the personality description is always more properly described by moving forward one sign in the zodiac and combining its influence with the ascending sign.

Another explanation might be that though the exact sign of the Ascendant is important, the Ascendant with the other stellar bodies move forward by direction each year so that if at birth, you had 23 degrees of Capricorn rising by about age seven, the ascending degree would have moved into Aquarius. Many astrologers have noted that there are definite changes in a person's life when the Sun changes sign by direction.

The Ascendant, of course, works in similar fashion. Although such direction is not usually indicative of a major event in a person's life, the personality definitely evolves into the characteristics of the next sign when such direction takes place. So a person born in the early degrees of a rising sign would in young adult life conform to that 'rising sign' personality. Most people by age 20 or so have reached the next sign on the Ascendant and definitely act like it. This knowledge is helpful in rectifying unknown birth times. Based on a person's personality expression in adult life, the unknown rising sign can be judged by selecting the sign preceding that sign which the adult is obviously expressing in the present. This may also apply to changes affecting personality traits when the Moon, Venus and Mars change signs by direction.

This is mainly important in chart delineation as it is always the degree on the natal Ascendant that is affected by transits and directions. When Chiron contacts the Ascendant by transit we often find just what we would expect – changes in the environment. This transit is especially evident at moves to a new location or changes of schools. It also signifies changes in family relationships and is often found in family member's charts when births and deaths occur.

The A/CH midpoint acts very much like the Ascendant combined with the other outer planets. When A/CH is contacted during a transit there will be some event in the family that has some noticeable affect. With A/UR something sudden, exciting or unexpected occurs in the family and with A/SA family difficulties are shown. With A/CH the change in the family situation is not as sudden or exciting as with Uranus nor as difficult as with Saturn. When a transit or direction contacts A/CH, it often breaks up an impasse or stalemate in the family. In other words it tends to get the family out of a rut. Sometimes it indicates some excitement in the neighborhood. Major transits to the A/CH midpoint often represent the arrival of a new person in the family, not in the usual sense of a birth or adoption but of someone well-known by the family moving closer.

Chiron and the Midheaven

The Midheaven may be considered the most important point in any person's chart. It is so significant that it is well worth trying to rectify a chart to locate it. The Midheaven represents the inner you as opposed to the outer which is shown by the Ascendant. Some call it the heart, others the soul, but whichever term is used it usually represents what is most important to you. It is also related to personal success and is related to career or love when involved in midpoints. In genealogical work it is the most important contact point in relationships.

Many astrologers have stated that the Midheaven represents the mother in one's chart and the opposite point, the IC, the father, and sometimes the reverse. The former works in practice and this point frequently depicts the children in a parent's chart. The Midheaven and the Midheaven midpoints are always connected so deeply and personally between charts in relationships that one could rightly conclude the presence of a "soul link." This seems to be true whether the relationship is between parents and children, spouses, friends or siblings. However, a transit of Chiron to the Midheaven usually means a change in relationship in relation to someone important in your life. It can be a happy or difficult change depending on whether you are losing or gaining someone. One woman had Chiron to the Midheaven on the day she learned of her mother's terminal cancer. I have also seen Chiron contact the Midheaven in births and it is prominent in family members' charts in cases of adoption.

The Chiron Midheaven midpoint when contacted by other planets and points by transit and direction is more often linked to one's career. It usually signifies a turning point for the better. Sometimes it will mean a turn for the better in a relationship.

Chiron and the M/A

The M/A/midpoint is also extremely important and second to the Midheaven in significance. Ebertin refers to it as the "point of the soul" and says that transits and directions to it represent very important periods in one's life. This point is especially important in chart comparison and contacts of the M/A in one chart to a personal point in another's indicate a definite link between them. The individuals involved understand each other without even speaking. Unfortunately transiting Chiron contacting the M/A is frequently seen on the actual day of a final grant of divorce. Transits of Pluto and PL/CH to the radical M/A are very strong and usually show a turning point in life. Chiron touching the M/A signifies a change in one's feelings or outlook and a change in one's environment. Transits and directions of Chiron here are common in moves and job changes. There is an interesting correlation between this point and the 165° angle. I have seen transits by this angle to the M/A bring important events into life while to other midpoints there was little observable effect. Like planets, midpoints may also have an affinity for certain angles not in common use. This would be a fruitful area for further research.

Altogether Chiron contacts to these three personal points represent areas in the chart that when touched by transits and directions indicate major soul growth experiences.

Chiron to Chiron

We should not leave this chapter without mentioning contacts of Chiron to Chiron. We have observed previously that these contacts are often by transit the triggers for major life events in direction such as births, deaths, and changes in relationships. It is a good idea when one of these transits is to occur to observe carefully the nearby directions and transits for clues as to what type of event to expect. Chiron passing rapidly by itself in a chart is not too important but in the case where Chiron because of retrograde motion, touches its natal position three times, then one of these contacts will surely signal something major in one's life.

When Chiron by transit touches a regular midpoint it seems to act just like the outer planets. In other words it combines with the meaning of the midpoint it aspects. However when by transit Chiron touches itself, the inner planets and especially the personal points of the Ascendant, Midheaven or M/A midpoint, the same types of events are experienced over and over again. These involve births, deaths, moves, job and relationship changes. Notice that they all involve some type of transition in relationships with others, the loss or gain of family members, friends, work associates or neighbors. There is sometimes a little variation such as a health crisis with the Sun, children with the Moon or new jobs with Mars, but on the whole all of the events represent some kind of turning point in life. In some way it either adds or takes away and sometimes both. In any event, life is changed in some irreversible way. There is no turning back. It is both a lock on the past and a new door to the future. The contacts of Chiron to these inner planets and personal points represent a transition in relationships. Note that Chiron is like a bridge between Saturn and Uranus. It partakes of the nature of both. That is why these contacts can seem so difficult. The Saturn component of a door closing is never an easy lesson. But, with Chiron, we also have the Uranian component. Something else is there and we must take a new direction. Perhaps that's why Al Morrison refers to it as an inconvenient benefic. It breaks up the stalemates in our lives. It raises our consciousness by taking us away from the past, healing old wounds, and like a teacher leads us into new relationships, to the next level of consciousness and the next phase of life. Chiron is the bridge from the past to the future. Chiron is the NOW.

Endnotes:

1. Debbi Kempton-Smith, *Secrets From a Stargazer's Notebook* (New York: Bantam Books, 1982), p.244.

2. Michel Gauquelin, *Cosmic Influences on Human Behavior: The Planetary Factors in Personality*, trans. Joyce E. Clemow (New York: ASI Publications, 1978).

8

Synastry

"You saw me before I was born and scheduled each day of
my life before I began to breathe. Every day was recorded
in your Book."

Psalms 139:16

In the previous chapters, Chiron's action by transit was examined
and its use in rectification discussed. In this chapter, we look more
closely at Chiron's influence in the natal chart or cosmogram as it's
effects in chart comparison and synastry have been strongly noted.
This is one area in which additional insights into Chiron can be found.
The use of Chiron in synastry work is particularly conducive to reveal-
ing the deeper significance of this mysterious body in astrological research. This is a logical development which follows naturally from
Chiron's powerful binding effects in human relationships.

The Cosmogram
Since the nature of how Chiron works with the other planets in
transits and directions is now known it should not be too big of a step
to carry that insight over into the natal chart or as we call it in cosmobiology, the cosmogram. Naturally if Chiron aspects a planet or point
in the natal chart one can assume that it refers to a transition or turning
point or breakthrough in life related which is related to the meaning of
the aspected planet and its place in the overall cosmic picture. Along
with this Chiron's role in decision-making was pointed out above.
Therefore, whenever Chiron aspects a planet in the natal chart some
key decision will have to be made. Each day you have many choices to

make. Which door will you take? These decisions will be faced when a Chiron aspect is activated by transits and directions. I have a good friend with Chiron in aspect to Uranus on the Ascendant. Throughout her entire life she has had to make instant decisions and judgments about about matters upon which her whole future depended. With combinations such as these one is not allowed the luxury of time to mull things over.

A good way to get a feel for Chiron in the natal chart is by looking at Chiron in the natal midpoint structure pattern. We spoke of these midpoint structure patterns earlier. They are essentially main midpoints from the natal chart grouped around the planets they are close to by degree. So in addition to checking Chiron's basic aspects in the chart, it is important to see which midpoints surround natal Chiron. If, for example, one finds CH = A/MN in the natal chart, it can be deduced that there will be a transition or turning point in the family or that unusual decisions will have to be made concerning the environment with others. Chiron to Mars/Pluto (CH = MA/PL) might mean success in an unusual career or a career "breakthrough" at some point in life.

The other thing to consider in the midpoint structures is the Chiron combinations with other factors that are listed under the other planets and points. For example, under Venus you might see MA/CH (VE = MA/CH). This could mean, among other things, a turning point with a male in a situation concerning art or love. A logical procedure in drawing such conclusions is to use key words which help draw relevant ideas together and then see how these results work in actual delineation.

Synastry and Chiron

Chart comparison or synastry is an excellent way in which to study human relationships. The use of midpoints is crucial in this work and not only has Chiron given many additional insights into its basic nature, but more has been uncovered by using this body in chart comparison. In her book, *The Continuing Discovery of Chiron*,[1] Erminie Lantero, quotes from a letter from Al H. Morrison, the publisher of CAO Times,

"Chiron in one natal chart conjunct or square any planet in some-
body else's chart confers the Chiron person with the ability to be a
total scourge or pain-in-the-ass in all efforts at relationship, and
perhaps the inability to be anything gentler, all with the best inten-
tions in the world."

I don't know how he came to this conclusion but I have found it to
be absolutely true! This may indicate a hidden side to Chiron. Indeed
the Chiron person in this situation could be described as a maverick in
the relationship. The Chiron person seems absolutely drawn to the
other yet at the same time to resists any development of intimacy. In
almost a yo- yo fashion this maverick Chiron person keeps popping
back into the other's life but as soon as he senses things getting too
"close" he tends to withdraw again. This kind of response is often seen
in chart comparisons, especially when the Chiron contact in one chart
is to a personal point in the other chart such as the Midheaven or
Ascendant. A person whose Chiron contacts a personal point in
another's chart may reflect like a mirror the behavior of the non-
Chiron person in their relationship to others. The Chiron person may
act as a teacher to awaken the non-Chiron person to a another side of
their own personality. In other words, the Chiron person gives the
other a taste of his own medicine by treating this person as he treats
others.

On the other hand this provides a clue as to the types of relationships to expect with Chiron contacts. Chiron may represent a different
kind of relationship than one would normally assume. Whatever the
answer, Chiron plays an important role in certain relationship patterns,
which is unlike any archetypal roles of the past. In chart comparison
Chiron is a like the MN in that it shows a "connection" or a karmic tie
with another. But there the similarity ends. A better understanding of
Chiron's role in such matters can be found by including its midpoints
in chart comparison.

Midpoints in Synastry

One of the best ways to study relationships is by comparing midpoints including those involving Chiron. Start by listing all the mid-

points and planets in the charts under consideration. First take one person's planets and personal points and see which points and midpoints they touch in the other person's chart. Then reverse the procedure with the other person's chart. Use as small an orb as possible, no more than a degree but preferably under 30'. It will be much easier to find the semisquares and sesquiquadrates contacts using a 45° sort. This procedure can be used for love relationships, business associations, family ties and friendships. In each there are specific things to be looked for depending on the type of relationship being investigated. The CSI is helpful in giving an idea of the meanings of the contacts between the various factors and midpoints. Keep in mind that both charts in which midpoints and planets are in mutual contact exactly, that is within a few minutes of arc, will be affected simultaneously by the same transits. For example, if one person's Venus is at 9 Cancer 48 and the other's SU/VE midpoint is at 24 Leo 50 (= 9° 50' Cardinal) then both Venus and the others SU/VE will be contacted at the same time by any transit to that point. It makes little difference in cosmobiology whether the contacting aspects are conjunct, square, opposite, semisquare, or sesquiquadrate. The mutual contact is what is important in cosmobiology not the kind of aspect they make. Nor is the sign in which these contacts occur of any particular significance when using midpoints. In the previous example, one person's Venus at 9 Cancer 48 and the others SU/VE at 24 Leo 50 would be shown as 9° 48' and 9° 50' in the 45° sort. Instead of saying therefore that Person A's Venus is semisquare Person B's SU/VE we would list:

Person A		Person B
Venus	=	Sun/Venus

After going through each person's chart and finding close contacts between them, they can be listed as follows.

Person A		Person B
VE	=	SU/VE
A	=	M
VE/MA	=	VE

80

MA	=	SA
MO	=	MO/PL
MA/JU	=	SU

This list is not inclusive as there are usually many more contacts in close relationships.

Love Relationships

In love relationships there are some very important things to look for. Ebertin in one of his books mentions a curious thing when comparing the charts of lovers. He found that the VE/MA midpoint of both was located in the same place. This is easily seen locate if a 45° sort is used. Taking this further one can say that the combinations of VE = VE/MA and MA = VE/MA are often mutually common in these types of charts. It is not that the relationship can't be solid without these contacts but that these common pictures are highly indicative of a very strong physical attraction which may not always be necessarily healthy. In her books, Karen Savalan[2] explores these concepts further.

If when comparing charts of love relationships you find few if any contacts or at most a few insignificant ones this does not bode well for a successful relationship. However if the contact potential is weak you normally won't see their charts because they wouldn't have gotten so far as to have formed a relationship in the first place. Occasionally though these weak comparisons can be seen very early in a relationship.

Besides the Venus/Mars contacts there is another clue often found in happy relationships and that is when one of the planets or sensitive points in the midpoint of one person's chart touches one of the same points or planets in the others chart.

Example:

Person A		Person B
VE	=	SU/VE
MA	=	VE/MA
MO	=	A/MO
VE	=	VE/UR
PL	=	MO/PL

This indicates a close affinity between the partners especially if their charts contain the personal points or the Sun, Moon or Venus. In a more detailed study interwoven patterns involving midpoint structures in both charts can be found. That is where the same planet or point is part of both midpoints.

Example:

Sun/**Mars**	=	Venus/**Mars**
Moon/Pluto	=	**Moon**/Venus
MN/Mars	=	**MN**/Venus
Sun/**A**	=	**A**/Moon

In comparing love relationships the most influential midpoints involve the SU, MO, VE, MA, A, M, and MN with any planet. In particular, MN combinations are often quite indicative of close ties. Another midpoint, MA/JU, is particularly useful in chart comparison and it is important if someone's MA/JU midpoint touches another chart in a positive way. In fact any exact contact between major planets, not including midpoints, is very strong. The other outer planets are not as important, unless they are touching a personal planet or point or a midpoint containing same. Pluto is particularly found in relationships that seem fated. Neptune and Saturn contacts can be quite problematical for successful relationships. Let's take as an example certain midpoints from the charts of one couple:

Tim		Joan
MO/VE	=	MO/PL
VE	=	VE/MA
MA	=	SA
SA	=	VE
SU/VE	=	SU
A	=	M
VE/UR	=	MA

From just a glance at these midpoints we can see a strong feeling of love and a deep physical attraction between the two. The VE/UR to MA contact usually means a lot of excitement in love and also a physical relationship. We have already discussed the VE/MA type of contact. The Ascendant of one partner to the Midheaven of the other also shows a strong spiritual bond or soul link and the SU to SU/VE contact is very positive. Yet through a strange series of events this couple eventually parted. This is a partial listing of their contacts. There were many other positive contacts of a different nature between their charts. Despite the many positive contacts which brought them together we can readily see how a couple of the contacts can be disastrous for any love relationship. The Saturn to Venus contact could add stability to the relationship, but it usually means that one party in the relationship will cause the other sorrow in love. This is exacerbated by the Mars to Saturn contact. Ebertin in *Cosmic Marriage* says of this combination, " a harsh fate, becoming separated." So it is wise then to look at the whole picture when comparing charts. These do not have to always mean the couple will break up but it does auger many problems for the relationship. Sometimes if couples have difficult aspects such as Saturn in one to Mars/Saturn in the other it may just mean "shared difficulties" rather than separation. It is more serious when a difficult midpoint or planet contacts a personal point or the Sun, Moon, or Venus as in the previous case than when just two "bad" midpoints or points contact each other. However, two difficult midpoints touching is not as significant. I once studied the charts of 50 couples and compared the main contacts between their charts. Besides the very prevalent Venus to Mars type of contacts the most common in order of predominance were: Sun to Ascendant, Venus to Ascendant, Moon to Ascendant, Sun to Venus, MN to Ascendant, Moon to the Midheaven, Moon to the MN and various combinations of these same points and planets. So far I've observed Chiron as increasingly important in chart comparison especially in contact to the A, M, MN, MO, SU and VE. One of the most successful and unusual relationships I've seen had Chiron = Midheaven as the main contact to a personal point. Chiron contacts so far seem to indicate where a partner will open doors for you to new ways of looking at the world and yourself. All of the ramifications of Chiron have certainly not been studied, however it clearly seems to play an important role in love relationships. I have often seen transiting Chiron stationary on important points in the beginning of a relationship or at the first meeting and sometimes later at turning points in the relationship between the couple. Even if the exact times of birth are not known meaning the positions of the Moon, Ascendant and Midheaven are uncertain, a great deal can be learned from a noon or solar midpoint chart.

Family Synastry

The synastry of family relationships is particularly fascinating. There are midpoints in abundance among family members and those involving the MN are especially interesting and important. These are common and are useful in rectification. If a father's MN is at, say, 23°05' of a mutable sign and a son's M/MN midpoint is near it then it is often possible to find the exact degree of the Midheaven because family contacts between charts are so close. Some of these same contacts are found in marriage relationships. These close ties cemented by the same kinds of midpoints structures are found in biologically related family members and also in the charts of in-laws; hence they do not necessarily indicate blood relationships. They do indicate fated relationships, however – those people you seem destined to spend many years with. Adopted children and their adoptive families should also be connected by these same types of MN connections.

There are several ways of looking at contacts among family members. One is to look at what is described herein as "family centers." The other is by comparing individual contacts between family members. There are usually many of these "centers" in any family's charts. What you have essentially is a midpoint that is exact to about a minute of orb for each person in the family in which the midpoints have similar meanings. Of course this implies that every transit contacting this central point will affect each family member at the same time. You will often find one of these such centers are readily observable and operable during a major event that affects the whole family. Let's take a look at one example: The common midpoint or "family center" was at about 11°33' in the 45° sort.

Family Center

Father	JU/PL 11°33'
Mother	MO/MN 11°34'
Child	MO 11°36'
Child	M 11°32'
Child	A/ME 11°33'

From these one would expect a sad or difficult family situation to occur on the day this point would be transited by NE/CH. On the other hand, much happiness could be expected for a child or female member of the household on the day of the transit by UR/PL or UR/-CH. Importantly these "family centers" will often include close relatives not sharing the same residence such as grandparents, aunts and cousins.

Ties

Among any group of family members there is an incredible array of similar contact points which indicate common ties between the charts. These are like the "centers" but are more limited in that they will touch just two people in the family. These are the individual contacts indicative of "ties." All combinations of the MN are extremely important points of contact between family members. Also very common and almost as important is Mercury. Mercury in these cases often indicates a child relative, brother, sister or cousin and occasionally brothers- and sisters-in-law. Both M/MN and A/MN are most often found in these instances. Often seen are combinations between members, such as:

Person A	to	Person B
MN		=M/MN
M		=M/MN
MN		=A/MN
A		=A/MN
MN/SA		=MN
MN		=MN/SA

85

MN/SA is also of major import; it indicates the karmic ties that might exist in which there would be difficult problems to work out in the relationship. A few examples follow.

> Girl's SU/MN = Brother's Sun or MA/MN
> Boy's MN/MA = Sister's or Aunt's VE/MN
> Aunt's MN/ME = Nephew's MO/MN

SU/JU, SU/MA and especially SU/ME are very prevalent between the male members of families and combinations involving the Moon, Venus and the Midheaven are common between females. Jupiter is also often frequently involved in combinations. Here is an example of one woman's contacts with her family members.

> A woman's MO = her mother's M
> M = her brother's Mars
> A = her father's Sun
> Sun = her uncle's MN
> MO = her sister's MN/M
> MO/MN = her sister's M

Combinations involving the personal points and planets and especially the MN are the most frequently found. A family member might have the M to anothers MN, A, SU, MO, VE, or MA or any combination of these factors.

Friends

The analysis of the charts of friends are equally interesting but are interpreted in a slightly different manner than those relating people by family or love. The most common points of contact are planets such as the Sun, Mars, Venus and Mercury. There is less contact shown by the Moon, and the MN in combinations such as VE/MA and SU/VE which denote romantic or physical love. Among friendships among males we see combinations of the Sun and either Jupiter, Mercury or Mars. Mercury is especially prominent with friends with whom you just "hit it off with." Between friends there is less contact involving the

86

personal points. Among friends we often find MA/JU contacts. Business associates important to you will have many of the same types of contacts as friends with special emphasis on Mars and Jupiter. All in all these contacts indicate an overall plan for our lives with very definite important relationships extending from the closest to the most distant and all having a karmic or 'destined' element to them. You either have something to learn from these people or something to teach them. The synastry between charts shows where we "touch" each other.

Chiron

Earlier in this chapter we mentioned how Chiron sometimes acts like MN in synastry. For example, a woman's SU/MN midpoint might be on her brother's Mars. This indicates a male related to her. A transit touching her brother's Mars affects him directly and at the same time touches her SU/MN, reflecting an event involving a male relative. Chiron in one chart touching a midpoint in another's acts in a very similar way. That is, it often points out the nature of the relationship. We can see this in the following list of examples:

M - Male: F - Female:

M CH	= his mother's A/M
F CH	= her niece's Mercury
F CH	= her sister's MO/PL
F CH	= her uncle's Mercury
M CH	= his aunt's Jupiter
F CH	= her mother's Ascendant
M CH	= his sister's ME/MA
M CH	= his sister's MO/UR
M CH	= his niece's SU/ME
M CH	= his aunt's ME/M
M CH	= his sister-in-law's M
F CH	= her younger brother's MO/JU
M CH	= his son's MO
F CH	= her son's CH/M
F CH	= her brother's MO/MN
M CH	= his brother's ME/VE

```
M CH    = his wife's MA/MN
M CH    = his father's VE/A
F CH    = her brother-in-law's MO/A
F CH    = her brother-in-law's CH/A
M CH    = his brother's A/M
F CH    = her nephew's ME/MA
M CH    = his wife's M
```

From this list we can gather that Chiron contacts between charts undoubtedly represent the nature of relationships. In synastry, then Chiron speaks more of the kind of relationship rather than just of relationship per se. When all the votes are in, Chiron will rule relationships that are of an unusual or unique character. These might include, for example, a teacher-student relationship not so much in the usual academic sense as in the spiritual sense.

Endnotes:
1. Al H. Morrison, as quoted by Erminie Lantero, *The Continuing Discovery of Chiron* (York Beach, ME: Samuel Weiser, 1983),p.52, n.26.

2. Karen Savalan, *Midpoint Synastry Simplified* (n.p.: by the author, 1979) and *Midpoint Love Simplified* (ibid., 1980).

9

A Time For Chiron

"There is a time for everything. A time
to be born and a time to die..."
                Ecclesiastes 3:1-2

Chiron and Cosmobiology

This volume is an humble attempt to look at Chiron, a newly discovered heavenly body, now considered to be of major astrological significance. It was shown how Chiron acts in the manner of the outer planets. Its effects in the horoscope by transits and in midpoint structures were discussed as well as its dynamic action in directions and in synastry. It remains to discuss other facets of Chiron which can increase our understanding of this small, but powerful astrological influence. It was brought out how Chiron may be a "planet" to herald a "the new age" in man's history, a period of new frontiers in many areas such as government, medicine, science and, yes, astrology. It was remarked that astrology today may be undergoing a turning point, a period of changeover from the dark ages where it has been a hidden, slightly off-beat area of interest only to those who had the courage and insight to leave the beaten path themselves. Over the centuries however astrology took a backseat and became divorced from astronomy, biology and medicine. It became not a science but a body of confusing superstitions full of fanciful illusions. Yet somewhere hidden under the accumulated debris of centuries was a golden nugget of truth. In this century many have spotted this nugget and have tried to dust it off, polish it and return astrology to the science it once was. Some of the newer social sciences like psychology and sociology along with holistic approaches to medicine and health are, in a sense, partakers of what astrology was originally all about — the study of man in relation to the cosmos and the laws of nature.

Whether it is called astrology, cosmobiology or some new term yet to be minted, this field of inquiry was not able to develop properly the way sciences did until this century when the tools of modern technology were made available. The development of the computer has especially revolutionized the toil of computation formerly involved. Observations and calculations that would have taken days and weeks can now be done in a flash. So it should not be surprising that the computer explosion crops up again and again in relation to Chiron. The nuclear field didn't need a representative planet like Pluto before this century, neither did electricity before Uranus or chemistry before Neptune. So Chiron may not have been needed until we were able, with the help of modern technology, to grasp the amazing scientific truth of cosmobiology.

Now that Chiron has been discovered and its mythology and psychological import is impressed on mass consciousness, the transition of astrology into the next century may take place. A door is now closing on the dark ages of superstition in which astrology survived and another is opening — the door of science. This will not take place without pain and upheaval, but take place it will. There can be no turning back. We can't unlearn knowledge. We can only try to handle it and control its use. More and more scientists now are discovering the interrelatedness of all life on earth. Perhaps with the use of this new science of cosmobiology they will also see our interrelationship with the cosmos as a fact of nature.

It may be that Chiron, among other things, may rule cosmobiology as Neptune rules chemistry. More mundanely, as an expression of daily life, Chiron represents transitions, breakthroughs, and turning points, and has a special affinity for relationships and healing. Chiron is a teacher for the new age that brings everything together.

Rulership

But what sign shall we assign to Chiron? This matter is still open to debate. Astrologers have associated it with just about every sign of the zodiac. Some have speculated that it rules no particular sign but instead serves as a catalyst with the other planets. As of now, the generally accepted rulerships of the zodiacal signs are as follows.

Sun   - Leo
Moon   - Cancer
Mercury   - Gemini and Virgo
Venus   - Taurus and Libra
Mars   - Aries
Jupiter   - Sagittarius
Saturn   - Capricorn
Uranus   - Aquarius
Neptune   - Pisces
Pluto   - Scorpio
Chiron   - ?

There is still some small dispute about the assigned rulerships of the three most recently discovered planets. It may not matter whether Chiron is assigned a rulership or not but if such an assignment should in time evolve Chiron will most likely replace one of the two planets which currently rule over two signs. Libra has already received much attention and with good reason. Chiron has a definite association with relationships, ruled by Libra. Its orbit even represents a good Libran compromise between Saturn and Uranus, vacillating between first one and then the other before striking a middle ground. Another possible assignment is over Virgo. Many astrologers suspect that Vulcan will soon be assigned to Virgo; Chiron may turn out to be the planet they are seeking. Virgo represents the analyst, the pure scientist and the practical application of science. Most assuredly, Gemini, the fleet--footed communicator, belongs where it is under Mercury's rulership. Virgo, unlike Gemini is more of a ponderer, philosopher and deep thinker, and not a communicator. Virgo is also related to healing, another area strongly associated with Chiron. Virgo represents individual service to mankind. But new ideals of service have now evolved, in which we all do our part in contributing some form of service to our fellowman. To truly serve to perfection, Virgo would need the tools of modern science — no sloppy, vague thinking admissible here.

This question of rulership will be narrowed down eventually. If Virgo wins out that leaves Libra and Taurus with Venus. But is it really that way? For most astrologers there is no doubt that Venus, the planet of love and peace, rules Libra. Its rulership over Taurus, which is grounded in the material, physical universe — the earth is confusing and is not clearly understood. The recognition of Chiron as the ruler of Virgo may not come swiftly. Virgo, ever humble, is usually the last to receive recognition. How closely the image of Chiron, the wounded healer, parallels the mythology of Vulcan, the lame god who serves.

Chiron and Biology

Another area of interest is Chiron's place in medical astrology. The other signs and planets have shown a definite affinity for certain part of the body. Uranus plays a big part in accidents and Mars is often associated with fevers and injuries or wounds. Chiron has some affinity with the environment and environmentally related diseases. It is probably strongly associated with the human immune system. It would be very interesting to see whether Chiron is strongly or difficultly placed in the charts of those afflicted with AIDS. This horrible disease is unlike any we have had to cope with in history and may require a whole new outlook in treatment. We are entering a "new age" in medicine. Rather than just the immune system Chiron may signify the entire area of holistic medicine and health care. Chiron is also associated with time - specifically a turning point in time. Perhaps it is time to look at the whole person and not just his "parts." It is a time for healing, not just for ourselves, but for healing our planet as well. It's time for Chiron.

Keywords Associated with Chiron

Breakthrough

Bridge

Catalyst

Coming Together

Common Ground

Doorway

Healer

Key

Link

Maverick

Relationships

Synthesis

Teacher

Time

Transition

Turning Point

Quick Chiron Midpoint Reference

Transiting Chiron Midpoints
(PL/CH)$_t$ major powerful turning point
(UR/CH)$_t$ thrilling turn of events
(NE/CH)$_t$ dissolving door
(SA/CH)$_t$ facing facts
(JU/CH)$_t$ fortunate change
(MN/CH)$_t$ turning tides

Other Transiting Midpoints
(UR/PL)$_t$ joy
(UR/NE)$_t$ unbelievable
(NE/PL)$_t$ unreal
(SA/UR)$_t$ tension
(SA/PL)$_t$ difficulty
(SA/NE)$_t$ angst
(SA/MN)$_t$ separation from or difficulty with others
(JU/UR)$_t$ sudden good luck
(JU/NE)$_t$ daydreaming
(JU/PL)$_t$ fortunate
(JU/MN)$_t$ happy with others
(UR/MN)$_t$ excitement with others
(PL/MN)$_t$ large group activities
(NE/MN)$_t$ association with sick, unhappy with others
(CH/MN)$_t$ group turning points

Other Midpoints with Chiron
(SU/CH)$_t$ breakthrough for male associate
(MO/CH)$_t$ feelings of excitement, child or female
(ME/CH)$_t$ news that changes things
(VE/CH)$_t$ turning points for loved ones
(MA/CH)$_t$ changes affecting a male
(CH/M)$_t$ turning point in career, soul experiences
(CH/A)$_t$ turning points in family or environment

Bibliography

Carter, Charles, *The Principles of Astrology*, Theosophical Publishing House, Wheaton, IL, 1963.

Ebertin, Reinhold, *The Combination of Stellar Influences*,
    Directions
    The Contact Cosmogram
    Applied Cosmobiology
    Cosmic Marriage
    The Annual Diagram as an Aid in Life
    Transits

All recent translated editions of these books available from the American Federation of Astrologers,Inc.,Tempe, AZ.

Gauquelin, Michel, *Cosmic Influences on Human Behavior: The Planetary Factors in Personality.* Translated by Joyce E. Clemow. ASI Publishers, Inc., 1978.

Grant, Ernest and Catherine T., *Predictive Astrology*, American Federation of Astrologers,Inc.,Tempe, AZ, 1988.

Greaves, Doris E., *Cosmobiology: A Modern Approach to Astrology*, American Federation of Astrologers, Inc.,Tempe, AZ, 1980.

Hand, Robert, *Planets in Transit*, Para Research, Inc. Rockport, MA,1976.

Hieratic Publishing Co., *The Complete Planetary Ephemeris for 1950-2000 A.D. at Midnight.* Medford, MA: Hieratic 1975.

Hone, Margaret, *Applied Astrology*, L.N. Fowler and Co.,LTD., England, 1983.

Kimmel, Eleonara, *Fundamentals of Cosmobiology (Revised)*, American Federation of Astrologers, Inc.,Tempe, AZ, 1979.

Lantero,Erminie, *The Continuing Discovery of Chiron*, Samuel Weiser, Inc., York Beach, ME, 1983.

Michelson,Neil, *The American Ephemeris for the 20th Century*, ACS, Publications, Inc., San Diego, CA, 1988.

Michelson, Neil, *The American Midpoint Ephemeris 1986-1990*, ACS, Publications, Inc., San Diego, CA, 1985.

Millard, Margaret M.D., *Casenotes of a Medical Astrologer*, Samuel Weiser, Inc., York Beach, ME, 1980.

Morrison, Al H., *Chiron Ephemeris*, computed by E. Gregory, CAO Times, New York, NY, 1985.

Savalan, Karen O., *Midpoint Synastry Simplified*. By the Author, 1979.

Savalan, Karen O., *Midpoint Love Simplified*. By the Author, 1980.

Smith, Debbi Kempton, *Secrets from a Stargazers Notebook*, Bantam Books, New York, NY, 1982.

Stein, Zane B. *Essence and Application: A View from Chiron*, CAO Times, New York, NY, 1988.

Tyl, Noel, *The Expanded Present, Vol.6, The Principles and Practice of Astrology*, Llewellyn Publications, St. Paul, MN, 1974.

Tyl, Noel, *Times to Come, Vol.12, The Principles and Practice of Astrology*, Llewellyn Publications, St. Paul, MN, 1978.

This first edition of Midpoint Keys to Chiron
was typeset and designed using WordPerfect,
a registered trademark of WordPerfect Corporation.
Body typeface is Marin 11 supplied by Publisher's Powerpak,
a registered trademark of Atech Software.